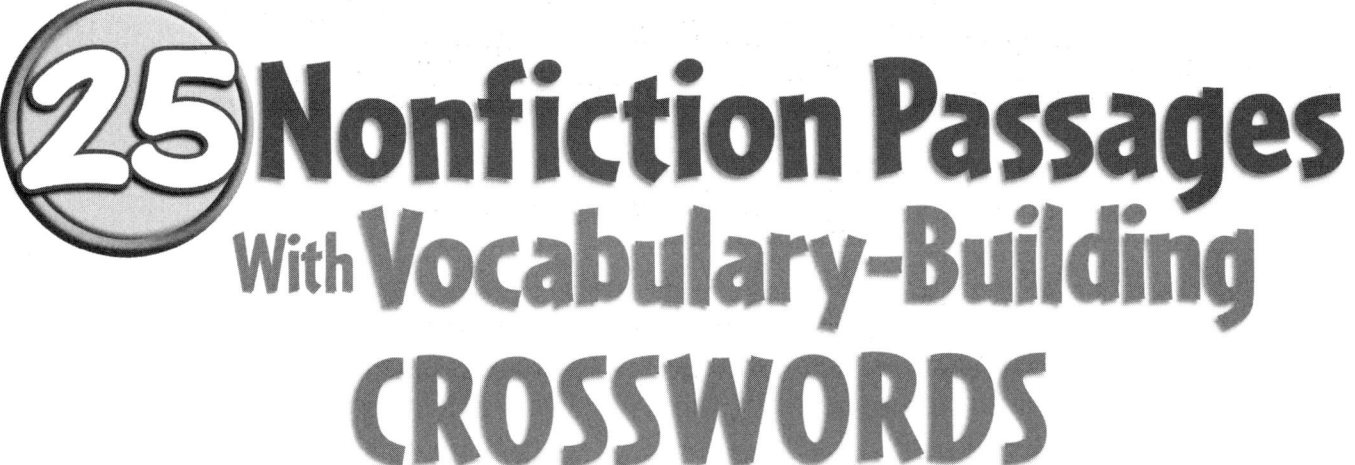

by Jan Meyer

NEW YORK • TORONTO • LONDON • AUCKLAND • SYDNEY
MEXICO CITY • NEW DELHI • HONG KONG • BUENOS AIRES

Teaching Resources

For Marilyn,
Jeff, Jennifer, Lisa,
and Steve

"Disappearing Frogs," "Journey Into the Earth," and "Mammoth Search" are adapted from SUPER SCIENCE. Copyright © 2005 by Scholastic Inc. Reprinted by permission.

Scholastic Inc. grants teachers permission to photocopy the designated reproducible pages from this book for classroom use. No other part of this publication may be reproduced in whole or in part, or stored in a retrieval system, or transmitted in any form or by any means, electronic, mechanical, photocopying, recording, or otherwise, without written permission of the publisher. For information regarding permission, write to Scholastic Inc., 557 Broadway, New York, NY 10012.

Cover design by Jason Robinson
Interior design by OPS, LLC
Interior illustrations by OPS, LLC

ISBN-13 978-0-439-46857-2
ISBN-10 0-439-46857-4

Copyright © 2006 by Jan Meyer. All rights reserved.

Printed in the U.S.A.
 2 3 4 5 6 7 8 9 10   40   14 13 12 11 10 09 08 07

Contents

Introduction 4
Nonfiction Passages
   Ancient Roman Baths 6
   Harry Houdini: Master of Escapes 8
   Mountain Gorillas 10
   The White House 12
   The Globe Theater 14
   Disappearing Frogs 16
   Margaret Bourke-White 18
   Life on Coral Reefs 20
   The Pony Express 22
   The Story Painter 24
   Treasures of Tutankhamun 26
   The Tin Lizzie 28
   Totem Poles 30
   Roberto Clemente 32
   Journey Into the Earth 34
   Bird Nests 36
   A Medieval Feast 38
   "Crazy Bet": A Civil War Spy 40
   History of the Yo-Yo 42
   A Man of the Wilderness 44
   The Incas 46
   Snakes: Hunters and Hunted 48
   The California Gold Rush 50
   Mammoth Search 52
   An American Hero 54
Narratives Word List 56
Word Whiz Word List 59
Answers 61

Introduction

About This Book

This reproducible classroom supplement is a fun and involving way to help students learn new vocabulary words and strengthen their skills in decoding word meanings. The high-interest narratives present 300 vocabulary words in context. The accompanying crossword puzzles let students test their understanding of these words.

The narratives, covering a wide variety of topics, are filled with fascinating and surprising facts. Each contains 12 vocabulary words printed in boldface type. Encourage students to look for context clues in the passages that will help them figure out the meanings of these words. As they find such clues in surrounding information, they will see that this is often a simple and effective way to determine the meanings of unfamiliar words.

The companion crossword puzzles help students master the vocabulary words. Each crossword clue is the definition of one of the boldfaced words as used in the paired narrative. Students will enjoy completing these puzzles and seeing whether they figured out the meanings of the words correctly.

Following each crossword puzzle is a special Word Whiz section that introduces additional vocabulary words—a total of 157 in all. Featured in many of these sections are words formed from prefixes, suffixes, and word roots. Students read the meanings of these word elements and the definitions for selected words containing them. Becoming familiar with these word parts and seeing how they can be used to unlock the meanings of words provides students with another important tool to use in building their vocabularies.

For your convenience, the Narratives Word List and the Word Whiz Word List each contain cross-reference page numbers to help you target particular words.

Activities to Reinforce and Extend Learning

Here are some activities that you may want to use to help students apply and become comfortable with the words they are learning.

When students have finished a narrative and the companion crossword puzzle, ask them to

- identify the part of speech for each of the words as used in the narrative.
- write sentences using each of the words from the narrative or a creative paragraph using all of the words from the narrative. (You may want to include words from the Word Whiz section as well.)
- use a thesaurus to find synonyms for selected words from the narrative and the Word Whiz section.
- use a dictionary to find other forms of selected words (adjective, noun, adverb, and verb). For example: abolish, abolition, abolitionist; or persist, persistent, persistence, persistently, persistency.
- make an index card for each word from the narrative that includes part of speech, definition, and a sentence using the word.

To provide additional practice in vocabulary-boosting skills, have students

- identify the clues they used to help them figure out the meanings of selected words from the narratives.
- use a dictionary to find additional words using the prefixes from the Word Whiz sections.
- use a dictionary to find out the meanings of additional prefixes and of some of the words formed from these prefixes. For example: bi-, inter-, mis-, sub-, super-, trans-, tri-.
- try to determine the meanings of the word parts found in these vocabulary words contained in the narratives (see the chart below).

audible (14)	aud-	hear
illuminate (14)	-lumin-	light
collaborate (18)	-labor-	work
transported (22)	-port-	carry
contemporary (28)	-temp-	time
incredible (32)	-cred-	believe
suspending (36)	-pend-	hang
novices (42)	nov-	new
descendant (46)	-scend-	climb
minimum (54)	mini-	small

Ancient Roman Baths

In ancient Rome, a visit to the public baths was an important part of daily life. Most large towns had at least one bath, and the city of Rome had many of them. The largest baths could **accommodate** more than a thousand bathers at a time. Many were **ornate** structures that had carved marble columns, statues, and floors with beautiful patterns made with small colored tiles. The public bath was more than a place to get clean. People also went there to **encounter** friends, gossip, have business meetings, exercise, read quietly, or have a snack.

Both men and women went to the baths, but they usually bathed in separate areas or at different times of the day. Most men visited the bathhouse in the afternoon when their work was finished. They left their **garments** on a shelf in the changing room, often paying a guard to make sure that these belongings were not stolen. Then, they might go to the exercise yard to wrestle, box, lift weights, or play a ball game. Hot and sweaty from this **strenuous** exercise, they were now ready to relax and get clean in the bathing area.

There was no set order for using the rooms of the bath building. However, most visitors **commenced** their bathing by sitting for a short time in the warm room called the *tepidarium*. Next, they went to the *caldarium*. This very hot, steamy room was heated by underground furnaces that sent hot air under the floor and up through the walls. In the *caldarium*, bathers might **recline** on a bench or soak in a hot pool. The Romans had no soap. To clean their bodies, they had bath attendants or their own personal slaves rub them with olive oil and then scrape away the **grime** and perspiration with curved metal scrapers.

Finally, to **conclude** their bathing and cool off, they went to the *frigidarium*. In this room, they could take a dip in a very cold pool. The bathers were now clean and refreshed. After getting dressed, they might play a dice game with their friends, buy a honey cake, watch a juggler, and then **stroll** in the gardens.

The baths could be a very **boisterous** place. Visitors liked to sing and whistle and shout to their friends. Added to this were the loud calls of food **vendors** and hair-pluckers looking for customers. The Romans loved the baths and believed that going regularly helped them to enjoy good health.

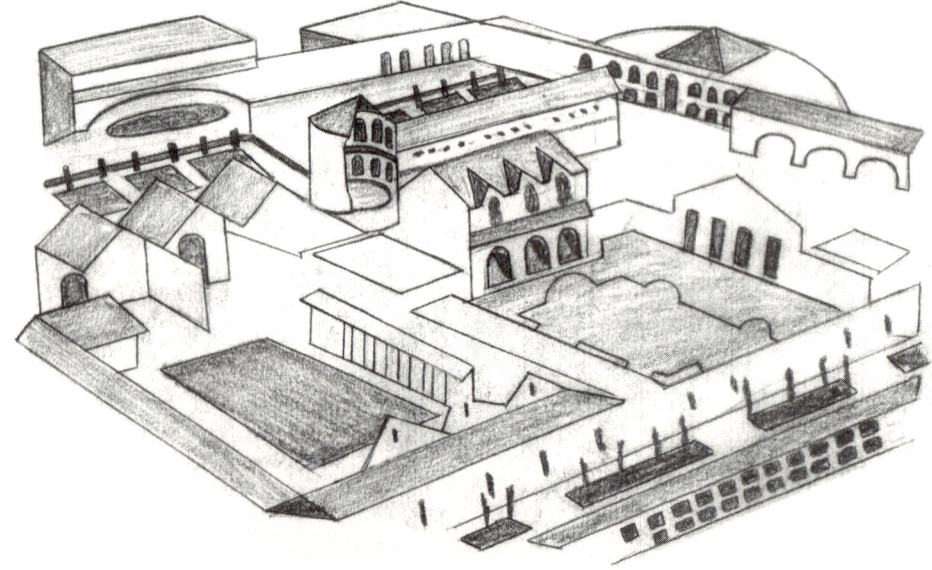

Crossword Puzzle

Complete the puzzle by filling in the vocabulary words that fit the definitions.

ACROSS
4. to have room or space for
5. dirt that has been rubbed into the surface of the skin
7. to bring to an end, finish
9. very loud and noisy, rowdy
10. to lean or lie back
11. sellers of goods

DOWN
1. to come upon or meet by chance
2. began, started
3. to take a pleasant, unhurried walk
5. articles of clothing
6. very active, requiring much energy or effort
8. filled with rich decorations

WORD WHIZ

The ancient Roman baths were called *thermae*. In our language we have the word roots **therm-** and **thermo-**. These roots mean "heat." Some words with these roots are

thermometer: an instrument for measuring temperature
thermostat: a device used to regulate temperature, especially for a heating unit or system

The adjective **thermal** means "having to do with heat." **Thermal** underwear is winter underwear that is made of special materials designed to keep the body warm.

Some other words associated with the Roman baths and with Latin, the language of the ancient Romans, are **frigid** (very cold), **tepid** (slightly warm, lukewarm), and **scald** (to burn with hot liquid or steam).

Name: _____   Date: _____

Harry Houdini: Master of Escapes

On an evening in 1918, a 10,000-pound elephant named Jennie was led into a cabinet on the stage of the Hippodrome, a theater in New York City. Harry Houdini, the world-famous magician, closed the cabinet's curtain. Several seconds later, he whipped open the curtain. Jennie had **vanished**! The theater **resounded** with the audiences' cheers and applause.

Houdini's real name was Ehrich Weiss. He was born in Hungary but moved to America with his family when he was quite young. To help pay family bills, he shined shoes and delivered newspapers. When he was 14, Weiss took a job cutting fabric for neckties. At night, he read books on magic and practiced tricks. A few years later, he quit this job to **pursue** his dream of becoming a magician. It was then that he changed his name to Harry Houdini, in honor of his hero Robert-Houdin, a **renowned** French magician.

Although he performed wherever and whenever he could, Houdini was not an instant success. In 1899, his luck changed when he made escaping from handcuffs a featured part of his show. He **extricated** himself from handcuffs fastened in front or back, from leg irons, and even from thick chains that locked his wrists to his ankles. Houdini, now billed as the Handcuff King, was becoming a star.

Houdini was always looking for new ways to **astound** his audiences. In 1908, he introduced a feature called The Water Can into his act. For this trick, he was handcuffed and squeezed into a large metal milk can that was filled to the top with water. The lid was fastened with locks and then a screen was placed in front of the can. To **dramatize** the danger, an assistant stood by with a fire axe, ready to smash open the can. The minutes ticked by on a large stage clock, increasing the audiences' nervousness. At last, a breathless and dripping Houdini **emerged** from behind the screen. The milk can, it was revealed, was still **intact** and locked. To prepare for this stunt, Houdini had **submerged** himself in his large bathtub at home and practiced holding his breath for increasingly long periods of time.

What were the secrets of Houdini's magic? Many of them will never be known. What we do know is that he had an extremely strong and **agile** body, a fearless spirit, and an unending drive to succeed. It was these **assets** and years of hard work that helped to make Houdini the greatest magician and escape artist of his time.

Name: _____   Date: _____

Crossword Puzzle

Complete the puzzle by filling in the vocabulary words that fit the definitions.

Across
5. to surprise greatly, amaze
6. to follow, seek actively
7. disappeared, went suddenly out of sight
9. things having value, advantages
10. with no part missing
12. was filled with sound

Down
1. to show in a dramatic way, make seem very exciting
2. set free, released
3. put under water
4. having great fame
8. appeared, came out into view
11. able to move with quickness and ease

Word Whiz

The word **dramatize** ends with the suffix **-ize**. This suffix can mean "to make," "to become," or "to cause to be." Some other words that end with this suffix are

equalize: to make equal or even
verbalize: to make verbal, to express in spoken words
fantasize: to create fantasies or imaginative ideas, to daydream about
brutalize: to make or become brutal or violent, to treat in a cruel manner

The suffix **-fy** can also mean "to make" or "to become." Some words with this suffix are

purify: to make pure or clean or not mixed with anything else
simplify: to make simpler, to make easier to understand or do

9

Mountain Gorillas

On the slopes of central Africa's Virunga Mountains and in nearby Bwindi Park, there are forests filled with **dense** growths of trees and plants that are green year round. Mountain gorillas, members of the great ape family, live in these misty, rainy forests. Because their **habitat** is cool during the day and cold at night, these gorillas have hair that is longer and thicker than that of their close relatives, the lowland gorillas.

A full-grown male mountain gorilla can weigh over 400 pounds. Because his back is covered with silvery hair, he is called a silverback. Although he is powerful, he has a **placid** nature. He leads his family to food, plays patiently with his youngsters, and rarely fights. He behaves in an **intimidating** way only when he feels threatened. Then he will roar, stand upright, bare his teeth, and beat his chest with his hands to show his **supremacy**.

The adult female is much smaller, weighing about 200 pounds. She is a **conscientious** and loving mother who cradles and protects her newborn in her arms. When she travels, her tiny baby clings tightly to the hair on her chest. When the baby is older, it rides on her back.

Mountain gorillas live in small family groups, headed by a silverback. The group spends much of its time feeding on the plentiful **vegetation** of the forest. An adult male often **devours** more than 50 pounds of such things as berries, thistles, roots, stems, shoots, and leaves in a single day. At midday, after a morning of wandering and eating, the group stops and rests. They groom each other, picking out burrs and insects. Then the adults lie down on the ground and **doze**. The youngsters chase each other, wrestle, and climb trees. When the silverback awakens, the group moves on to **forage** for more food. They walk on all fours, resting their weight on the soles of their feet and the knuckles of their hands. At night, they make leafy nests on or close to the ground in a sleeping place chosen by the silverback.

There are many sounds, **gestures**, and facial expressions that mountain gorillas use to communicate with each other. They smack their lips, pat the ground, chuckle, and grunt. When they are resting and feel contented, they make a soft belching sound.

With only about 650 left in the world, mountain gorillas are endangered. A number of organizations, aware of their **plight**, are working hard to protect them from hunters and save their forest homes from loggers and farmers. Only if their efforts are successful will these peaceful apes live on.

Name: _____ Date: _____

Crossword Puzzle

Complete the puzzle by filling in the vocabulary words that fit the definitions.

Across
2. sad or dangerous situation
6. eats up in a hungry or greedy way
8. peaceful, calm, quiet
9. go about searching for food
10. frightening
12. always taking care to do the right thing

Down
1. place where an animal or plant naturally lives
3. motions made with a part of the body to express an idea or feeling
4. supreme power or authority
5. plant life
7. sleep lightly
11. thick, closely packed together

Word Whiz

Mountain gorillas are **diurnal**. A diurnal animal is active during the day. Here are some other words that tell about the behavior of particular animals:

nocturnal: Nocturnal animals are active during the night.
carnivore: Carnivores are animals that feed on the meat (flesh) of other animals.
insectivore: Insectivores are animals that feed mainly on insects.
herbivore: Herbivores are animals that feed on grasses or other plants.
omnivorous: Omnivorous animals eat both meat and plants.
scavenger: Animals that are scavengers feed on garbage and decaying matter such as the remains of animals.

The White House

Although George Washington directed the design and building of the White House, he never lived in it. The first President to **inhabit** the new presidential residence was John Adams. He and his wife, Abigail, moved to the mansion in 1800. When they arrived, they found nearly half of the rooms unfinished. The grounds were filled with construction **debris**, the roof leaked, and the house was cold and damp. The bathroom was a three-hole outhouse in the backyard and water had to be brought from almost half a mile away.

By 1809, when James Madison became President, the White House was much more comfortable. But five years later, during the War of 1812, it became a blackened ruin. British forces marched into Washington and set the White House on fire. The roof and the entire **interior** were totally destroyed. Fortunately, a sudden thunderstorm **extinguished** the flames and saved the outside walls. It took more than two years to rebuild the mansion.

In 1901, Teddy Roosevelt and his wife moved into the White House with their six children and a **diverse** collection of pets, including squirrels, a parrot, a kangaroo rat, and a snake named Emily Spinach. It was a lively time in the mansion. The **rambunctious** Roosevelt children walked on stilts in the gardens, raced in the hallways on roller skates, and sped down the grand staircase on trays. In 1902, the government approved funds to repair and add space to the overcrowded White House. The State Dining Room was made larger, new wiring was **installed**, and a West Wing with offices for the President and his staff was constructed. In the following 40 years, a full third floor was added to the residence, the East Wing was built, and the West Wing was enlarged to include the Oval Office.

During Harry Truman's presidency, the structure of the White House was found to be dangerously weak. It was agreed that only the outside walls, the roof, and the third floor could be **retained**. The rest of the mansion would have to be **dismantled** and completely rebuilt. In 1949, Congress approved an **expenditure** of $5.4 million for the work. When the **renovation** was finished, the White House had a bomb shelter, a movie theater, and more than 100 rooms. Since then, a bowling alley, an outdoor pool, and a jogging track have been added.

The White House has grown in size and changed with the times, yet it remains one of our nation's most important **symbols**. It continues to be, as described by Abigail Adams over 200 years ago, a house "built for ages to come."

Name: _____ Date: _____

Crossword Puzzle

Complete the puzzle by filling in the vocabulary words that fit the definitions.

Across
3. kept or held onto
5. taken apart
8. put in place for use
9. put out a fire or flame
11. amount of money spent
12. marks, designs, or objects that stand for or represent something else

Down
1. wild, noisy, rowdy
2. inside or inner part of something
4. to live in
6. different, not alike, varied
7. the act of restoring or making like new again
10. broken, scattered remains

Word Whiz

The word **renovation** begins with the prefix **re-**. This prefix can mean "again," "once more," or "anew." Some other words that start with this prefix are

reunite: to bring or come together again (to unite again)
redistribute: to give out in shares again, to divide among several or many again (to distribute again)
reevaluate: to determine or decide the value or worth of again (to evaluate again)
reoccur: to happen or take place again (to occur again)
reinsert: to put, set, or fit into again (to insert again)
readmit: to let in or allow to enter again (to admit again)

13

Name: _____   Date: _____

The Globe Theater

The Globe Theater, built in 1599, was one of England's first public playhouses. It was **situated** near the south bank of the Thames River, across from the city of London. William Shakespeare, the famous playwright, was one of the theater's **initial** owners. The stage of the Globe is where many of Shakespeare's plays were first presented.

The theater was a large building, open to the sky in the center. Because there were no gas or electric lights to **illuminate** the stage, all plays were performed in the afternoon. Both the rich and the poor attended these **matinees**. For a penny, those with little money could stand in the open-air courtyard on the sides and in front of the stage. This group, known as groundlings, **jostled** each other for a good view. Around the courtyard rose **tiers** of wooden benches, covered by a roof. That is where wealthier playgoers sat. The very rich sat on cushioned seats in boxes close to the stage. Thieves wandered about, hoping to steal money purses. They looked for **unwary** people in the crowd who were busy watching the play.

When it was full, the Globe held several thousand playgoers. The audience could be very noisy. They ate snacks and often chatted with each other during a performance. If they were bored by a play, the groundlings **jeered** and sometimes threw fruit at the actors.

The stage was a large, raised platform on which there was no scenery. Instead, props, furniture, music, and sound effects were used to help the audience imagine the settings and actions of the scenes. A lighted candle or torch was carried in to suggest nighttime. A loud rumbling of drums was used to **simulate** thunder. Cannons were fired to add excitement to a battle. Costumes were very important and were made of the most expensive materials. They were stored in the tiring house, a closed area behind the stage that also served as a dressing room.

The Globe's company of actors had to be **versatile**. They performed many different roles in the course of a month. An actor had to be able to fight with swords, dance, learn his lines quickly, and speak in a strong, expressive voice that was **audible** to everyone in the theater. Women weren't allowed to act in plays, so female roles were always played by boys.

In 1642, the English government passed a law that **prohibited** the performance of plays. Although the Globe was torn down two years later, Shakespeare's plays lived on and are now presented in theaters all over the world.

Name: _____ Date: _____

Crossword Puzzle

Complete the puzzle by filling in the vocabulary words that fit the definitions.

Across

3. made fun of in a rude way
7. to sound, look, or act like
9. to light up, give light to
10. disallowed or prevented from happening by an order or a law
11. performances held in the afternoon
12. pushed or shoved in a rough way

Down

1. located, placed
2. able to do a number of things well
4. series of rows placed one above another
5. loud enough to be heard
6. first, beginning, earliest
8. not watchful, careless

Word Whiz

The word **matinee** came into our language from the French language. Here are some other words that entered English from the French language:

detour: a road that is used when the main road is blocked or closed to traffic
acrobat: a performer skilled in such feats as tightrope walking, swinging from a trapeze, and tumbling
intrigue: a crafty plot or secret plan
amateur: a person who does something without much skill
souvenir: an object kept as a reminder of something
debut: a first public appearance

Name: _____ Date: _____

Disappearing Frogs

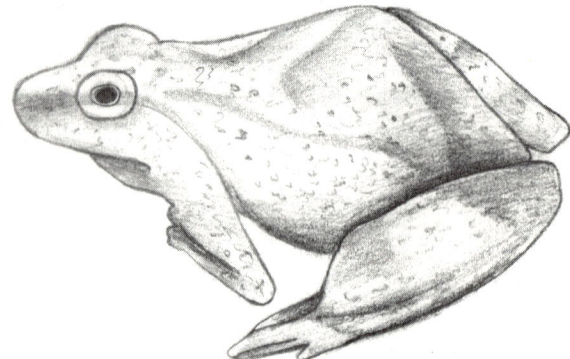

Unlike humans, frogs don't drink water. Instead, they **absorb** it through their skin. Most of it soaks through a "seat patch" on their bottoms when they sit on **moist** ground. At one time in the Monteverde Cloud Forest **Reserve** in Costa Rica, frogs could depend on the clouds that hung around the mountains to keep the forest floor wet and the mountain streams flowing.

When Earth's water **evaporates** from oceans, lakes, or puddles, changing from liquid to water **vapor**, clouds form. The water vapor rises when heated by the sun. In Monteverde, the water vapor used to rise until it ran into cold air around the mountaintops. This cold air condensed the vapor into liquid water droplets. The droplets then **clumped** together to make clouds. When clouds **blanketed** the mountain, the droplets gathered to make the little pools of water that the frogs needed.

In recent years, the air temperature in Monteverde has increased. Often the air around the mountaintops is too warm to **condense** the water vapor, so it keeps rising until clouds form high above the mountains instead of on the mountaintops. As a result, the land below dries out. This condition has proven **dangerous** for the frogs. Now, they have a hard time finding the water they need on the forest floor, and this is why the frog population is decreasing.

Most scientists believe that people are causing many places on Earth to get warmer, including Monteverde. They call the process global warming. People often add to global warming by burning fuels such as oil, natural gas, and coal. These fuels power almost everything we plug in or drive. As the fuels are burned, a gas called carbon dioxide is given off. Carbon dioxide occurs naturally in our **atmosphere**. It helps to keep Earth warm by holding in the sun's heat. But having too much carbon dioxide in the air is like throwing a heavy blanket around the planet—it keeps in too much of the sun's heat, and the world gets warmer.

High cloud formation caused by global warming is a serious problem. And according to scientists, it adds to the growing list of troubles that the wildlife of Monteverde is faced with. The frogs and other wild animals there have to **cope** with many problems, such as habitat loss and disease, and adding global warming may push them over the edge to **extinction**.

There are things that you and your family can do to keep the world from getting warmer. For starters, encourage your family to use the car less. Also, turn off the lights and appliances that you aren't using. By becoming an Earth-friendly family, you'll help wildlife all around the world!

Name: _____ Date: _____

Crossword Puzzle

Complete the puzzle by filling in the vocabulary words that fit the definitions.

Across
1. changes from liquid to water vapor
5. to change from water vapor to liquid
7. deal with something successfully
8. thickly covered
9. slightly wet
11. likely to cause harm or injury

Down
1. no organisms of a species remain
2. layers of gas that surround a planet
3. to soak up
4. grouped together
6. protected place
10. a gas formed from a liquid or solid

Word Whiz

The word **dangerous** ends with the suffix **-ous**. This suffix can mean "full of." Something that is **dangerous** is "full of danger." Some other words that end with this suffix are

vigorous: energetic, strong, powerful (full of vigor)
humorous: very funny or amusing (full of humor)
furious: very angry (full of fury)
spacious: very roomy or large (full of space)
voluminous: of great size (full of volume)

The suffix **-ful** also means "full of." **Careful**, **hopeful**, **fearful**, **successful**, **painful**, and **powerful** all end with this suffix.

17

Margaret Bourke-White

Margaret Bourke-White loved the energy of industrial scenes, so she was **elated** when she was allowed to take photographs inside a Cleveland steel mill. It was a hard project. The heat from the blast furnaces was **intense** and there were difficult lighting problems to solve. Night after night, she climbed up hanging ladders to shoot down on the **molten** steel as it was being poured into molds. Finally, after many weeks of work, she had produced amazing photographs. The best of these pictures appeared in magazines all over the Midwest. With many now **acknowledging** Bourke-White's talent, her career as a photographer took off.

The following year, Bourke-White accepted an offer to work for *Fortune*, a new magazine about business and industry. It was 1929 and she was just 25 years old. For the **premiere** issue, she shot photographs at a meat-packing plant in Chicago. Her pictures showed **slaughtered** hogs hanging in rows, men carving cuts of meat, and even the huge mounds of pig dust that would be made into feed for other animals. For another assignment, she photographed the construction of a skyscraper. Always fearless, she clung to a beam 800 feet above the ground to get some of her views. In 1934, Fortune sent Bourke-White to the Great Plains to photograph the conditions caused by months of **drought**. She returned with pictures of dying cattle, choking dust storms, and crops **withering** in the fields.

Saddened by what she had seen, Bourke-White decided to give up industrial subjects and use her camera to record people and their lives. In 1936, she agreed to **collaborate** with the writer Erskin Caldwell on a book about poor people living in rural areas of the Deep South. That same year, she joined the staff of *Life*, a new magazine that would use series of photographs to tell important news stories. She worked for this magazine for about 20 years, focusing her camera on events all over the world.

During World War II, Bourke-White served as a war **correspondent**, working for both *Life* and the U.S. Armed Services. The horrors and dangers of war never **dissuaded** her from getting the pictures she wanted. She rode in the lead plane on a bombing mission, traveled with troops, and photographed the wounded in a medical tent close to enemy lines.

When she was a child, Bourke-White dreamed of one day doing things that women didn't do. With unending ambition and courage, she **fulfilled** that dream.

Name: _____   Date: _____

Crossword Puzzle

Complete the puzzle by filling in the vocabulary words that fit the definitions.

Across

3. someone who reports news from a particular place or region
5. killed for food
7. drying up, shriveling
9. melted, made liquid by heat
10. discouraged someone from doing something
11. recognizing or accepting to be true

Down

1. long period without rain
2. carried out, realized, satisfied
3. work together on something
4. presented for the first time
6. very strong, very great, extreme
8. happy, joyful

Word Whiz

The word **collaborate** begins with the prefix **col-**. The word **correspondent** begins with the prefix **cor-**. These prefixes, and the prefixes **co-**, **con-**, and **com-** mean "with" or "together." Some other words that start with these prefixes are

collide: to come together with force, crash into
compile: to put together in an orderly way
convene: to meet, to gather or call together
consolidate: to join together into one unit
confer: to meet together for a discussion, talk things over with others
compatible: able to get along well together

Life On Coral Reefs

Coral reefs are found in the warm, clear waters of tropical seas and oceans. The branching and mounded coral "rocks" of these reefs are built up from the skeletons of tiny coral animals that live joined together in **colonies**. Only the outer layers of these hard coral formations are made up of living coral animals.

Coral reefs **teem** with animal life. A great variety of fish swim about in the **tranquil** waters. Some of the most beautiful are the butterfly fish and angelfish. Their bright colors and interesting patterns of spots, stripes, and swirls help make the reefs look like colorful underwater gardens. Clams, sponges, shrimp, starfish, crabs, and many other kinds of sea creatures also **dwell** among the coral. Moray eels hide in dark **crevices**. When small fish swim by, the eels shoot out and catch them with their razor-sharp teeth. Sharks and barracudas **lurk** on the edges, hunting for food. Sea turtles stop by to rest and feed.

Some fish on these reefs have unusual ways of **evading** their enemies. The porcupine fish has sharp spines covering its body. When it senses danger, this fish can **inflate** its body by swallowing water. Puffed up like a prickly balloon, it may now be too big or look too unpleasant to eat. The four-eye butterfly fish uses **deceit** to avoid being eaten. It has a large, dark spot that looks like an eye on each side of its body near the tail fin. Confused enemies, mistaking the tail for the head, are fooled into attacking the fish from the rear. This gives the four-eye butterfly fish time to quickly swim forward and escape.

The sea horse is one of the oddest fish found on coral reefs. Its body is covered with bony plates and it has a long tail that it can wrap around underwater plants. To hide, the sea horse can **camouflage** itself by changing color to match its background. Unlike other fish, it swims upright, using a fin on its lower back to slowly move itself through the water.

Some human activities are harming coral reefs and threatening the fish and other sea creatures that live on them. Waste materials and oil spills that **contaminate** the waters, changes in ocean temperature, sea floor mining activities, and too many careless tourists can all cause damage. It is fortunate that people are starting to **preserve** these reefs and establish laws to protect their animal life.

Name: _____ Date: _____

Crossword Puzzle

Complete the puzzle by filling in the vocabulary words that fit the definitions.

Across

2. to wait out of sight in a sly way
5. to pollute, make dirty or foul
7. to live, reside
8. misleading representation, dishonest trick
10. to hide by blending in
11. to swell or puff out

Down

1. calm, peaceful
3. to keep safe, protect from harm
4. groups of the same kind of animal living together
5. narrow openings, cracks, splits
6. avoiding or escaping by cleverness
9. to be full of

Word Whiz

The word roots **aqua-** and **aque-** come from the Latin word *aqua*, meaning "water." Some words formed from these roots are

aqueduct: a large pipe or channel for bringing water from a distant place
aquarium: a tank or bowl in which fish are kept
aquanaut: an underwater explorer

The adjective **aquatic** means "living in or taking place in water." Swimming is an **aquatic** sport. A water lily is an **aquatic** plant.

The word **marine** means "of the sea." A dolphin is a marine animal. A **mariner** is a seaman or sailor.

The Pony Express

In March of 1860, a number of daring older boys responded to a newspaper ad that read: "Wanted: Young, skinny, wiry fellows not over eighteen. Must be expert riders willing to risk death daily. Orphans preferred." Those who were hired became riders for the Pony Express, a new business **venture** that started operation on April 3, 1860.

The freight-carrying firm of Russell, Majors, and Waddell established the Pony Express as an answer to California's need for faster mail delivery. Their postal service **transported** letters and telegrams along a nearly 2,000-mile trail between St. Joseph, Missouri, and Sacramento, California, and it did this in just ten days.

To set up their business, Russell and his partners hired about 80 riders, bought more than 400 horses, and established over 150 Pony Express relay stations. The selected ponies had to be fast and have the **stamina** to keep up a steady, full gallop over a rough trail. The riders had to be honest, dependable, and **undaunted** by danger.

The Pony Express operated day and night, even in storms, and ran east to west and west to east. Its delivery system was like a cross-country relay race. A rider began his shift by charging ahead on his pony to a relay station, a distance of about 15 miles. There was no time to **linger** over food or a drink. In less than three minutes, he had to swing up on a fresh pony and **resume** his hard and fast ride. After about 75 to 100 miles and, perhaps, five changes of horse, the **exhausted** rider could finally stop and rest. A new rider grabbed the saddlebag of mail, mounted a pony, and continued on.

Pony Express riders traveled across a difficult and dangerous **route**. On many stretches of the trail, riders faced the possibility of attack by wild animals, outlaws, or **hostile** Indians. As a **precaution** against these threats, they armed themselves with at least one gun. Crossing through the Sierra Nevada Mountains in California was particularly **hazardous**. One slip on a slick rock and the horse and his rider could fall into a canyon below.

The Pony Express made its last run in the late fall of 1861. It had been losing money and the need for its fast service had lessened. Telegraph wires had finally been laid all the way to California. The Pony Express lasted less than two years, but **legends** of the adventures of its brave riders are still heard and read today.

Name: _____ Date: _____

Crossword Puzzle

Complete the puzzle by filling in the vocabulary words that fit the definitions.

Across
4. to stay on or be slow in leaving
5. very tired, worn out
7. strength or energy to keep going
8. to start again
9. care or action taken ahead of time to avoid a possible danger
10. stories handed down from the past
11. dangerous, full of risk

Down
1. not afraid, not discouraged
2. carried from one place to another
3. undertaking or activity in which there is a risk of losing something
6. unfriendly, acting like an enemy
8. course or road that is traveled to get to a place

Word Whiz

The word **precaution** begins with the prefix **pre-**. This prefix means "before in time." Some other words that start with this prefix are

prehistoric: of or belonging to a time before history was written down
predetermine: to decide or determine something beforehand
premature: happening or arriving before the expected time
preview: to show or view ahead of time
predate: to be or happen before in time, to come before

The prefix **post-** means "after in time."
Postwar means "having to do with the period after a war."

The Story Painter

The artist Jacob Lawrence has been called a story painter. That's because his art tells stories about the lives of African Americans from the years just before the Civil War through the 1900s.

Jacob Lawrence moved to New York City in 1930, when he was 13. He lived with his mother and two younger **siblings** in Harlem—a large and lively African-American neighborhood. It was in the community centers of Harlem that he received his early art training and heard about the **accomplishments** of African-American heroes such as Frederick Douglass and Sojourner Truth. Lawrence dropped out of high school so that he could help support his family, but he continued to paint and go to art classes whenever he could. Soon his work was being shown in Harlem art **exhibitions** and praised by community artists.

When he was about twenty, Lawrence began creating series of paintings using inexpensive poster paints on hardboard panels. Four of the groups that he painted tell stories about important events in the fight against the **injustice** of slavery. One of these is about the life of Harriet Tubman, the African American who helped more than 300 slaves make their **perilous** escape to the North on the Underground Railroad. Lawrence gave a number to each painting in these series and wrote a short description that **accompanied** each scene.

In 1940, Lawrence rented an unheated studio in Harlem for $8 a month. It was there that he painted his best-known series, The **Migration** of the American Negro. This group of 60 paintings **depicts** the flight of thousands of African Americans to the North during and after World War I. It was a story that had special meaning for Lawrence. His parents were among those who had left the South in this **quest** for jobs and a better life. As was typical of his art style, Lawrence used simple shapes and flat, **vivid** colors to paint each picture. Completed in 1941, when he was 23, the series won him national **acclaim**. That same year he became the first African-American artist to be represented by an important New York City art gallery.

Lawrence continued to create art until his death in the year 2000. In the last 10 years of his life, he won **numerous** awards including the National Medal of Arts, which was given to him by the President of the United States. Today, Lawrence's paintings are in the collections of nearly 200 museums.

Name: _____ Date: _____

Crossword Puzzle

Complete the puzzle by filling in the vocabulary words that fit the definitions.

Across
1. went along with
6. represents in a picture or pictures
8. dangerous
9. lack or absence of fairness
10. things requiring skill or determination that have been done successfully
11. brothers and/or sisters

Down
1. great praise, strong approval
2. movement from one place to settle in another place
3. public shows or displays
4. bright, strong, lively
5. very many
7. a search or hunt

Word Whiz

The word **injustice** begins with the prefix **in-**. This prefix can mean "not," "the opposite of," or "without." Some other words that start with this prefix are

inaccurate: not correct (not accurate)
insignificant: not of any importance (not significant)
involuntary: not done of one's own free will or choice (not voluntary)
ineligible: not having the qualities or conditions required, not qualified (not eligible)
insufficient: not enough, not as much as is needed or wanted (not sufficient)
incompetent: not having enough ability to do what is needed (not competent)

Treasures of Tutankhamun

Howard Carter, an English **archaeologist**, stood facing the sealed inner door to a royal tomb in Egypt's Valley of the Kings. It was November 26, 1922. With him was a rich English lord who was paying for Carter's work. They knew it was the tomb of Tutankhamun because there was an **impression** of his royal seal on the door. But they wondered whether the king's mummy and the many things buried with him for his afterlife would still be inside. Many of the tombs that had been discovered in the valley had been completely **looted** in ancient times by thieves looking for gold, gemstones, and costly perfumes. Carter cut an opening in the door and put a lighted candle through the hole. He was **astonished** by what he saw! Inside the room there was the glitter of gold and a **profusion** of objects heaped together in great piles.

Carter had first become interested in ancient Egypt when he was a boy. Convinced that Tutankhamun was buried somewhere in the valley, he had **persisted** in his search for the tomb for five years. It had been slow and **tedious** work. Year after year, Carter and his helpers had dug pits and ditches and cleared away tons of rocks and soil. At last, his efforts and the endless **excavating** had paid off.

The next day, the men entered the first of the four treasure-filled rooms they would find in the tomb. There were hundreds of objects crowded tightly together. Among these was a golden throne on which Tutankhamun must have sat when he **reigned** over Egypt—more than 3,000 years before. In an **adjacent** room there were even more riches. Carter soon realized that weeks of hard work lay ahead. Everything in the first room had to be photographed, recorded, and removed before they could examine the rest of the tomb.

It wasn't until February that they were able to enter the burial chamber and the small room beyond it. Within Tutankhamun's heavy stone coffin were three nested mummy cases, the last of which was made of solid gold. Inside this was the king's mummy, with **opulent** jewelry placed in the linen wrappings. Magic charms, **intended** to protect Tutankhamun as he traveled through the underworld, lay on the mummy. A beautiful gold mask covered the mummy's face. It captures the calm, youthful look of this king who died in his teens.

It took Carter many years to remove and pack every object found in the tomb. Most of these treasures are now in a museum in Cairo, Egypt. Tutankhamun still lies in his tomb in the Valley of the Kings.

Name: _____   Date: _____

Crossword Puzzle

Complete the puzzle by filling in the vocabulary words that fit the definitions.

Across
1. kept on trying, refused to give up
3. ruled as a king or queen
6. amazed, greatly surprised
8. robbed
9. someone who studies life in ancient times, especially by digging up old remains
11. meant for a particular purpose or use

Down
1. great amount, very large quantity
2. long and tiring
4. mark made by pressing or stamping
5. digging out or scooping out
7. next to or near by
10. costly, showing wealth and richness

Word Whiz

The suffix **-logy** means "the science or study of." An **archaeologist** is an expert in the science of **archaeology**. Here are some other words with this suffix:

geology: the scientific study of Earth's crust; including its soil, rocks, and minerals

meteorology: the scientific study of weather, climate, and Earth's atmosphere

psychology: the scientific study of the mind, the emotions, and human behavior

zoology: the scientific study of animals and animal life

paleontology: the scientific study of the forms of life that existed in prehistoric times as represented by fossils

The Tin Lizzie

Henry Ford was determined to build a "horseless carriage." Finally, after **persevering** for several years, he succeeded. In 1896, he pushed his gas-powered vehicle out of a shed behind his home in Detroit and drove off down the street. Ford called his car the Quadricycle because it ran on four bicycle wheels. Although everyone **marveled** at his car, it was not the first automobile in America. In fact, the **previous** year there had been a 54-mile road race in Chicago. The winning car had an average speed of about 7 miles per hour.

In the early 1900s, steam-powered cars and battery-powered electric cars were being built. But cars with gasoline-powered engines soon became the most popular. In this kind of engine, a mixture of gas and air **ignited** by electrical sparks burns inside metal cylinders. A long metal rod **transmits** the engine's power to the rear wheels.

Henry Ford continued to make cars and, in 1903, started the Ford Motor Company. He dreamed of producing a car that would be **affordable** for almost everyone. In late 1908, he introduced the Model T. **Affectionately** called the "Tin Lizzie," it was plain looking, sturdy, and easy to repair. It had a gas-powered engine and a top speed of 45 miles per hour. The Model T was an instant hit! In its first year, about 10,000 were made and sold.

The introductory price for the Model T was $850. Ford believed that by speeding up production he could lower this price. In 1910, the company moved to a large factory. There, Ford and his engineers continually tested new ways to make cars more **efficiently**. Production began to increase by nearly 100 percent each year. By 1914, the cars were being built on moving assembly lines. This was an entirely new way of making cars. Workers, standing at fixed positions, added **components** as car frames went slowly by on a moving belt. To save even more time, Ford began making the cars only in black. That year, a Model T cost about $500.

The Model T changed the lifestyles of millions of Americans. Farm families made shopping trips into towns. City families made weekend **excursions** to the country. Roads became **congested** with cars—well over half of them were Model Ts.

Then, in 1925, sales of the Model T began to drop. Car buyers wanted **contemporary** styling and features. The Model T's basic design had changed little since 1908, and it now seemed old-fashioned. On May 26, 1927, the 15 millionth Model T rolled off the assembly line. Soon after that, production of this well-loved car ended.

Name: _____   Date: _____

Crossword Puzzle

Complete the puzzle by filling in the vocabulary words that fit the definitions.

Across

5. lovingly, fondly
7. short trips taken for pleasure
9. modern, up-to-date
10. continuing to do something in spite of difficulties
11. was filled with wonder and amazement
12. set on fire

Down

1. producing results with the least possible time, energy, and effort
2. main or important parts of a whole
3. able to be paid for
4. coming or happening before
6. overcrowded, blocked up
8. sends from one place to another

Word Whiz

The word **transmits** comes from the Latin word *mittere*, which means "to send," or "to let go." Some other words with the word roots **-mit** and **-miss-** are

remit: to send in payment to a person or place
emit: to release, give off, send out
emissary: someone sent on a special errand, business, or duty
missile: a weapon or other object made to be shot or thrown at a target
submit: to give or hand in to someone to look over or decide about
omit: to leave out
dismiss: to send away, allow to go

Name: _____   Date: _____

Totem Poles

    The land along the coast of the Pacific Ocean stretching from southern Alaska down to the state of Washington was once dotted with Native American villages. It was in this region that Northwest Coast Indians made the carved wooden columns that we call totem poles.

    Carved figures representing humans and animals were arranged one above another on totem poles. These figures had special relationships with family **ancestors** and told stories about family histories. Some of the animals found on these poles were bears, killer whales, wolves, beavers, eagles, and ravens.

    Artists who were **proficient** carvers were usually hired to make totem poles. In the 1800s, when a great number of poles were made, the best artists were kept very busy. Most poles were made from red cedar, a tree that was **abundant** in the forests and was strong and easy to carve. Poles made from this wood could stand for about 50 years before they **deteriorated** from wood decay and fell to the ground. Paint made from crushed salmon eggs mixed with natural materials was used to **accentuate** important features of the carved figures. Red, black, and blue-green were the colors most commonly used.

    There were six main types of totem poles. Each was **erected** for a different purpose. House poles supported roof beams. Family poles, placed at the front of a house, usually had an opening through which the house could be entered. Welcoming poles, located on the beach, greeted guests arriving by canoe. Funeral poles held the remains of the **deceased**. Shame poles, often with an upside-down figure, were created to **humiliate** someone who owed a debt. Memorial poles stood in front of houses to **commemorate** chiefs who had died. Some poles, made from the tallest trees, could be more than 40 feet high.

    When the carving of a totem pole was completed, it was often raised at a party given by the owner of the pole. This celebration, called a potlatch, could last for days and included feasting, singing, dancing, and gift-giving by the **host**. Sometimes there were more than a hundred guests. To raise the pole, a deep hole was dug. Then a group of men, using ropes and poles, pushed, pulled, and lifted the **unwieldy** pole. When at last it stood upright for all to admire, the proud owner explained his totem pole and **recounted** the stories suggested by the figures on it.

30

Crossword Puzzle

Complete the puzzle by filling in the vocabulary words that fit the definitions.

Across
1. to call special attention to
6. not easily handled because of size or weight
7. to make someone feel ashamed
9. skillful, expert
10. put up, set in an upright position
11. became worn in condition or lower in quality

Down
2. to honor the memory of
3. those who come before one in a family line
4. existing in great quantity, plentiful
5. told about in detail
7. person who entertains guests
8. no longer living, dead

Word Whiz

The word **unwieldy** begins with the prefix **un-**. This prefix means "not" or "the opposite of." Many words begin with this prefix. The prefixes **il-**, **im-**, and **ir-** can also mean "not" or "the opposite of." Some words that start with these prefixes are

illiterate: unable to read or write (not literate)

illegible: very hard or impossible to read (not legible)

immobile: not moveable, firmly fixed (not mobile)

imprecise: not accurate, correct, or exact (not precise)

irrelevant: having nothing to do with the subject (not relevant)

irretrievable: impossible to recover or bring back (not retrievable)

Name: _____   Date: _____

Roberto Clemente

On a dusty lot in Barrio San Antón, Puerto Rico, some teenage boys were noisily **engaged** in batting practice. They were using a stick as a bat and old tin cans as balls. Señor Marín stood by his car, watching them play. He was looking for talent for a softball team to be sponsored by his **employer**, the Sello Rojo rice company. Soon, it was Roberto Clemente's turn to bat. He sent can after can flying to the ends of the lot. Señor Marín was amazed by this boy's **dynamic** batting performance. The next day, Clemente, just 14 years old, received his first baseball uniform: a red-and-white T-shirt with the rice company's name on it.

Four years later, Clemente was wearing the uniform of the Santurce Crabbers, a top team in Puerto Rico's Winter League. He had **attained** his dream of becoming a professional baseball player. At first, he didn't play much. But late in the season, he was given a chance to show the **spectators** in the stands what he could do. It was the ninth inning and the Crabbers' **opponents** were ahead by two points. The Crabbers had the bases loaded with two outs. Clemente came in as a pinch hitter, slammed the ball for a double, and batted in three runs.

On April 17, 1955, Roberto got his first major league hit. He was 20 years old and the new right fielder for the Pittsburgh Pirates. The fans soon noticed this player who always **endeavored** to do his very best. He hit smashing line drives, had a powerful throwing arm, and made **incredible** catches in right field. In a 1960 game, he ran headfirst into a concrete wall to make a catch. His jaw needed stitches, but he managed to hold on to the ball!

In 18 seasons with the Pirates, Clemente brought honor to himself and pride to the thousands of Puerto Ricans who **revered** this sports star from their island. He was the National League batting champion four times and the right field Gold Glove winner for 12 **consecutive** years. He was voted his league's Most Valuable Player in 1966 and World Series MVP in 1971. With a hit in a game on September 30, 1972, he met one of his most important career goals. He became the eleventh player in baseball history to have 3,000 major league hits.

Roberto Clemente died in a plane crash on New Year's Eve, 1972. He was on his way to Nicaragua to deliver food, clothing, and medical supplies to the **survivors** of an earthquake. Several months later, he was voted into baseball's Hall of Fame. This man who was so proud of his Puerto Rican roots became the first Hispanic to receive this **distinction**.

Name: _____   Date: _____

Crossword Puzzle

Complete the puzzle by filling in the vocabulary words that fit the definitions.

Across

1. full of power, energy, or force
5. people who watch an activity, onlookers
8. tried hard, made an effort
9. people that remain alive through a threatening situation
10. people who are on the other side in a game
11. taking part or involved

Down

1. honor
2. so amazing that it's hard to believe
3. company or business for whom someone works for pay
4. following directly one after the other
6. got by working hard
7. loved and greatly respected

Word Whiz

The word **spectator** comes from the Latin word *specere*, which means "to look" or "to look at." Some other words with the word root **spect-** are

spectacle: something to look at that is an unusual sight or a grand public show or display

spectacles: an old-fashioned name for eyeglasses

inspect: to look over carefully, to examine

The word root **-scope** is used in the names of many instruments that one looks through. Such instruments include the **telescope**, **microscope**, and **kaleidoscope**.

A **periscope** is an instrument that is used in submarines to get a view of the surface of the water.

Journey Into the Earth

Welcome to Lechuguilla in Carlsbad, New Mexico—the deepest and most dazzling cave in the United States. Scientists say Lechuguilla is about 1,632 feet deep, but new rooms and tunnels are constantly being discovered, causing the cave's measurements to get larger all the time.

The cave explorers who first discovered Lechuguilla in 1986 knew they had found something big. While digging into a desert pit, a howling wind blew out of the ground. The strength of the gust indicated that the wind had traveled far, so the cave underneath the pit was extremely long and deep.

Like most caves in Carlsbad, Lechuguilla is carved out of a rock called **limestone**. Most limestone caves get their start with rainwater. As rain falls through the air, it absorbs a gas called carbon dioxide. The rainwater then hits the ground and travels through the soil, where it gathers even more carbon dioxide. This water and carbon dioxide combination makes a fizzy acid that is just like soda water. As rainwater drips through cracks in the ground over thousands of years, the acid **dissolves** the limestone.

But Lechuguilla formed differently from its limestone neighbors. According to scientists, **microbes** live in the groundwater of Lechuguilla. These microbes ate a gas called hydrogen sulfide and then produced a very strong acid as a waste. This acid mixed with the water and then **seeped** into the rocks. After the acid-rich water drained out, it left the rock full of holes, like a big sponge or a piece of Swiss cheese.

Although Lechuguilla's caverns and passageways finished forming thousands of years ago, its spectacular **formations** are still growing and changing. As rainwater drips through holes in Lechuguilla's limestone ceiling, it dissolves rock that's filled with a **mineral** called calcium carbonate. As this mineral hardens, it forms into sharp **stalactites** that hang from the ceiling. A similar thing happens when the water hits the floor, though the effect is different: the mineral forms into **stalagmites** that shoot up like cones from the ground.

Lechuguilla is also filled with sparkling crystals. Because the water in the cave contains lots of minerals, when the water evaporates, it leaves these minerals behind on rock surfaces. These left-behind minerals **gradually** form giant, clear crystals that **jut** from the walls like swords or chandeliers.

The cool cave formations aren't the only features that attract scientists to Lechuguilla. Some researchers are interested in learning more about the microbes living in the cave. Certain microbes are used to create drugs that treat **infection** in humans, so scientists believe the tiny life-forms in caves may have medical **benefits**. Just think about it! There's an incredible world beneath our feet that hardly anybody knows about.

Name: _____   Date: _____

Crossword Puzzle

Complete the puzzle by filling in the vocabulary words that fit the definitions.

Across

2. seems to disappear when mixed with liquid
6. creatures too small to be seen by a naked eye
9. cave rocks that hang down from the cave's ceiling
10. an illness caused by germs or viruses
11. taking place slowly but steadily

Down

1. flowed or trickled slowly
3. cave rocks that stick up from the cave's floor
4. a fine-grained rock formed by layers of sediments squeezed and stuck together over a long period of time
5. objects made by the forces of nature
6. solid material found in nature that has particles arranged in a repeating pattern
7. something that helps
8. to stick out

Word Whiz

The word **benefits** begins with the word root **bene-** that means "well" or "good." Some other words with this word part are

beneficial: of good use, helpful, favorable
benefactor: a person who provides help to others, especially with gifts of money

The word root **mal-** means "bad" or "evil." Some words with this word part are

malevolent: showing ill will, wishing evil to happen to others
malign: to say bad or unkind things about
malady: an illness or unhealthy condition
malfunction: to function or perform badly, to fail to work as it should

35

Bird Nests

Most birds build nests to help keep their eggs warm and safe. To **ensure** the safety of these eggs, they must be careful where they make their nests. Some birds build nests in places so high that most **predators** can't reach them and eat the eggs. Others hide their nests in tall reeds, inside bushes, or in the thick, green **foliage** of trees. Kingfishers place their nests at the end of very long tunnels that they dig into riverbanks with their beaks.

Some birds make **elaborate** nests by weaving materials together. It is amazing that these birds, with no fingers to use, can make such nests. They **fashion** their woven nests by using their beaks. The male weaver bird of Africa begins its nest by **suspending** a knotted ring of grass from a tree branch. Then it weaves grass in and out until the nest is completed.

A few birds work together to build nests that they share. Social weavers, another kind of weaver bird found in Africa, pile dry grasses on the branches of a tree. Their nests **resemble** huge haystacks. More than 100 pairs of birds sometimes live in these "apartment houses" for birds.

The tailorbird sews leaves together to make a cup into which it can place its eggs. It **pierces** the edges of the leaves with its pointed beak. Then, using its beak as a needle, it stitches the leaves together with silk from spider webs or with plant materials.

Bald eagles make some of the largest nests found in the world. A male and female pair often work together to build their nest at the top of a tall tree or high on a rocky cliff. They **utilize** branches and sticks to form the structure and then grasses, feathers, moss, and pine needles to make a soft lining. The birds work **diligently** for several weeks or more collecting and placing all of these materials. A bald eagle nest is often used by the same male and female pair year after year. Each spring, the nest is repaired and new branches are added. After many years of use, the nest can become **immense**. One old bald eagle nest was found that measured about eight feet wide, nearly twenty feet high and weighed close to two tons!

There is even a bird nest that is **edible**. Swiftlets, found in Southeast Asia, nest deep inside caves. They use nothing but their own sticky spit to make their nests. The spit dries into hard, creamy-white cups that stick to the walls of the caves. These nests are often collected and used in China to make soup.

Name: _____ Date: _____

Crossword Puzzle

Complete the puzzle by filling in the vocabulary words that fit the definitions.

Across

1. extremely large
4. suitable or fit to be eaten
6. to make, form, shape
8. to look like, be similar to
10. animals that hunt, kill, and eat other animals
11. with a constant and hard-working effort
12. leaves of a tree or plant

Down

2. made with great care and detail
3. hanging down by attaching to something above
5. to make sure or certain
7. makes a hole in or through something
9. to make use of

Word Whiz

The Latin word for bird is *avis*. The English word **aviary** comes from this Latin word. An **aviary** is a large enclosure or cage in which birds are kept. The words **aviator** (a person who flies an airplane) and **aviation** (the science of operating aircraft) also come from *avis*.

Here are some other words related to birds:

plumage: the feathers of a bird
preen: to clean, smooth, and arrange the feathers with the beak
nestling: a baby bird that is too young to leave the nest
fledgling: a young bird that has just grown the feathers it needs for flying
talons: the claws of a bird of prey (an eagle or a hawk, for example)

A Medieval Feast

Step back into the thirteenth **century**, a time when the nobles of Europe lived in great stone castles that had tall towers and strong, protective walls. Let's visit one of these castles where preparations are being made for a **sumptuous** feast.

The head cook and under-cooks are **bustling** about the hot kitchen. Many courses will be served and there is much to do. Some servants are slicing fruits that will be cooked in wine. Others are plucking feathers from blackbirds, swans, and a peacock. Bread, fish, and meat pies are baking in the ovens. In the large open fireplace, the **carcass** of a wild boar is roasting on a spit, turned by a boy. Next to it, bubbling **cauldrons** filled with stews hang from chains over the fire. **Pungent** smells of garlic, onions, herbs, and spices fill the air.

In the castle's great hall, long tables and benches are being set up. At one end of this room is a table that is **elevated** on a platform. This table, called the high table, is where the lord of the castle, his family, and the most honored guests will sit. Cups, plates, bowls, and spoons are placed on the tables. The diners will bring their own knives.

At 10:30 A.M., a trumpet signals that the feast is about to begin. The guests, **attired** in their best clothes, wash their hands with perfumed water and then listen to a blessing. Breakfast was at sunup, so everyone is **ravenous**.

A parade of servants carries dishes into the hall from the kitchen. One of the most amazing of these is the roasted peacock. Its head, tail, and the rest of its colorful feathers have all been reattached. The carver cuts up the roasted meats and gives the best pieces to the diners at the high table. The cupbearer stands by to make sure that empty cups are quickly **replenished** with wine. Servers pass platters that are heaped high with food and ladle stew into bowls that are shared by each pair of guests. Since forks were rare in medieval times, the diners use their fingers to fish out tasty **morsels** of meat from the stews.

More and more courses are brought into the hall. The sweet dishes include fruit pies, a pudding with rose petals, and something called a subtlety. The subtlety, made with sugar and almond paste, has been molded to look just like the castle.

By the end of the feast, the lord and his guests have **consumed** great quantities of food. Many feel just as stuffed as we often do at the end of a very big Thanksgiving dinner.

Name: _____   Date: _____

Crossword Puzzle

Complete the puzzle by filling in the vocabulary words that fit the definitions.

Across
1. filled up again
4. period of 100 years
8. raised to a higher level
9. small pieces or bites of food
10. dressed up, clothed
11. very costly and fine, more than enough

Down
2. having a very sharp smell
3. ate or drank up
4. large kettles or pots
5. very hungry
6. busily hurrying
7. body of a dead animal

Word Whiz

The word **century** comes from the Latin word *centum*, which means "hundred." Another word that comes from this Latin word is

centennial: the 100th anniversary of an event

The Latin word *mille* means "thousand." A **millennium** is a period of 1,000 years.

The Greek word *deka* means "ten." Some words that come from this Greek word are

decade: a period of 10 years
decathlon: a track-and-field contest with ten different events including racing, jumping, and throwing the javelin
decapod: a crustacean with ten legs or arms, such as a crab, a shrimp, or a lobster

"Crazy Bet": A Civil War Spy

During the Civil War, women in the North and the South were eager to help in the war effort. They made uniforms, nursed the wounded, or took over the duties of their husbands who had left home to fight. Since only men could become soldiers, a small number of women **disguised** themselves as men and served on the battlefield. Others offered to act as spies for the Union (the North) or the Confederacy (the South).

Elizabeth Van Lew, a Southerner, was one of the most daring and successful spies for the North. She was born in 1818, in Richmond, Virginia. There, she lived with her **affluent** family in a beautiful mansion that was taken care of by household slaves. Unlike her father, she felt slavery was evil and should be **abolished**. In fact, after her father's death, she convinced her mother to free their slaves.

When the Civil War began, she was very **distressed**. She **vowed** that she would do everything she could to help the Union. Van Lew was known for being strange and she **shrewdly** used this as a cover for her spying activities. To **exaggerate** her oddness, she dressed in shabby clothes and mumbled to herself on the street. People called her "Crazy Bet" and disliked her views, but they never thought she could be a spy.

Van Lew became a frequent visitor at Richmond's Libby Prison where she took food to recently captured Union soldiers. The prisoners told her about Confederate troop activities they had seen on their way to prison. She also **obtained** important information from the prison commander. He liked to talk with this woman who brought him gingerbread.

Jefferson Davis, president of the Confederacy, was another source of information. He accepted her offer to send him a servant. Into his home went her former slave, Mary Elizabeth Bowser, who reported to Van Lew on the many military discussions she overheard.

Van Lew had a number of **schemes** for getting information to Union officers. The notes she sent out of Richmond were sometimes **concealed** in the hollowed-out heels of her messengers' shoes or tucked inside empty eggshells in baskets of food. She even created a secret code. She kept the key to this code in the back of her watch.

General Ulysses S. Grant was the **recipient** of many of her messages. At the end of the war, he visited Van Lew to **commend** her for her brave and valuable help to the Union. It is reported that she proudly kept his calling card for the rest of her life.

Name: _____ Date: _____

Crossword Puzzle

Complete the puzzle by filling in the vocabulary words that fit the definitions.

Across

3. cleverly or with a sharp mind
7. hidden, kept out of sight
9. to make something seem greater or larger than it really is
11. to praise
12. upset, troubled, saddened

Down

1. plans of action
2. rich, wealthy
4. hid true identity by changing appearance and clothing
5. someone who receives something
6. done away with, gotten rid of completely
8. got or gained by making an effort
10. made a serious promise or pledge

Word Whiz

Here are some words related to spies and spying:

espionage: the use of spies and secret agents by one country to find out about military and strategic secrets of other countries

cryptographer: someone who is an expert in putting messages into secret codes and in decoding messages put into secret codes by others

covert: done in a secret or hidden way

surveillance: a close watch kept over someone

eavesdrop: to listen to others talking when they don't know that they are being overheard

41

Name: _____   Date: _____

History of the Yo-Yo

The yo-yo is one of the world's oldest toys. No one is sure when or where it **originated**, but it is known that there were yo-yos in ancient Greece about 2,500 years ago. Among the **artifacts** in the National Museum of Athens, Greece, visitors can see a vase, from about 500 B.C., that shows a young boy with a yo-yo. Some of these ancient Greek yo-yos were decorated on their two halves with pictures of Greek gods.

In the late 1700s, the yo-yo made its way to England and France. At that time, a French artist painted a **portrait** of the young son of King Louis XVI holding his *l emigrette*, as the toy was called in France. In England, the yo-yo was known as a quiz, a bandalore, and a Prince of Wales' toy.

Pedro Flores is given credit for starting this spinning toy's rise in popularity in America. Flores grew up in the Philippines in the early 1900s. Like most children there, he learned to carve and **manipulate** a wooden toy called a "yo-yo." ("Yo-yo" means "come, come" in Tagalog, a language of the Philippines.)

Flores **immigrated** to the United States and took a job in California as a hotel bellhop. On his lunch breaks, he played with a yo-yo that he had carved. Often, crowds would **congregate** to watch him do tricks with his toy. Flores wanted to do well in his new country and **aspired** to work for himself. Making and selling yo-yos, he realized, might make this dream come true. In 1928, he started the Flores Yo-Yo Company. To increase sales, he helped yo-yo **novices** learn to do tricks and held spinning contests for yo-yo experts. The contest winners were those who could keep their yo-yos spinning for the longest **duration**.

In 1930, Donald F. Duncan, a smart businessman, bought the Flores Yo-Yo Company and **acquired** the rights to the name "yo-yo." Over the years, Duncan and other manufacturers have added new features that have helped to make the yo-yo one of the world's most popular toys.

The yo-yo traveled to one more new **destination** in 1987. It was taken into space on the Space Shuttle Discovery as part of NASA's Toys in Space project. There, the yo-yo was used in experiments on how toys behave in a weightless environment. It seems quite amazing that this ancient toy has **endured** long enough to have been played with in space.

Name: _____ Date: _____

Crossword Puzzle

Complete the puzzle by filling in the vocabulary words that fit the definitions.

Across

4. place to which a person or thing is going
6. to come together in a large group
7. man-made objects, often remaining from an earlier time or culture
9. came into a foreign country to live
10. lasted, continued, remained
11. gained or got as one's own

Down

1. had a desire or ambition for something
2. people new to something, beginners
3. handle with skill
4. length of time during which something continues
5. came into being
8. picture of a person, usually showing the face

Word Whiz

The prefixes **in-** and **im-** sometimes mean "in" or "into." The prefixes **e-** and **ex-** mean "out," "out of," or "from."

Pedro Flores **immigrated** to (came into) the United States. He **emigrated** from (moved out of) the Philippines.

The United States **imports** (brings in) bananas from Central America. Central America **exports** (sends out) bananas to the United States.

When something is **included** in a group, it is part of or in the group. When something is **excluded** from a group, it is kept out of the group.

A Man of the Wilderness

North of San Francisco there is a protected woods that contains a **grove** of coastal redwoods, one of the oldest and tallest trees on Earth. This national monument is named Muir Woods—a **tribute** to John Muir, a leader in the fight to save our nation's wilderness areas.

John Muir was born in Scotland in 1838. He and his family came to America in 1849 and settled in Wisconsin where they cleared land for a large farm. Muir had an **aptitude** for anything mechanical and loved to invent things. One of his most **ingenious** designs was a clock that attached to his bed. With the aid of wheels and levers, this "Early Riser" machine could tip him out of bed at a **designated** hour. Muir also loved nature. He spent any free time he had wandering through the fields and forests, watching birds. When he was 22, Muir left the farm and went to a fair in Madison, the state capital, to show his inventions. He stayed in Madison and **enrolled** at the University of Wisconsin.

In 1867, Muir, at work in a factory, suffered a serious eye injury that changed the direction of his life. While he was **recuperating**, he decided to give up inventing and spend his time exploring and studying nature. In early September of that year, he set out from Louisville, Kentucky, for a 1,000-mile walk through undeveloped land to the Gulf of Mexico.

The following year, Muir traveled by ship to California and then walked to Yosemite Valley in the Sierra Nevada Mountains. **Awed** by its beauty, he remained in this area for six years. He hiked to waterfalls, studied rocks and plants, discovered glaciers, and climbed to the **summits** of mountains.

When he was 41, Muir married and moved to a fruit-growing ranch near San Francisco. He often sat in his "scribble den," writing articles about what he had experienced and learned in the wilderness. Always **yearning** to wander in nature's wild places, Muir traveled whenever he could. On these trips, he was **appalled** to see increasing signs of land and forest destruction. Greatly concerned, he became a leading writer and speaker on the need to **conserve** natural resources and protect the nation's scenic wonders. Two important rewards for these efforts were the establishment of Yosemite and Sequoia national parks in 1890 and the setting aside of millions of acres as national forests and parks by President Theodore Roosevelt. Today, these beautiful places that Muir helped save can still be enjoyed.

Name: _____   Date: _____

Crossword Puzzle

Complete the puzzle by filling in the vocabulary words that fit the definitions.

Across
2. natural ability, quickness in understanding
6. recovering from a sickness or injury
9. highest points, tops
10. selected, chosen
11. registered, signed up to become a member
12. to keep from being lost, hurt, or wasted

Down
1. feeling a longing or desire
3. something given or done to show thanks or respect
4. shocked, greatly upset
5. cleverly planned or made
7. filled with wonder and respect
8. group of trees standing together

Word Whiz

The word **conserve** is a verb. It can be changed to the noun **conservation** by adding the suffix **-ation**. The suffixes **-ition** and **-ion** can also be used to change certain verbs to nouns. Some other nouns made with these suffixes are

donation: money or goods **donated** (given) to such things as a fund or a charity

vibration: the motion made when something **vibrates** (moves rapidly back and forth)

quotation: words from a person or a piece of writing that are **quoted** (repeated exactly as said or written)

definition: a statement that **defines** (makes clear or explains) the meaning of a word

allocation: a portion or share that is **allocated** (set aside) for a special purpose

Name: _____   Date: _____

The Incas

    The empire of the Incas **flourished** for only about 100 years, but it was one of the largest and richest ancient civilizations in the Americas. In the late 1430s, the Incas began to conquer neighboring tribes and put them under their control. At the peak of the empire's power, its lands **extended** nearly 2,500 miles along the western coast of South America. Much of this land was in the steep Andes Mountains.

    Life in the Inca Empire was organized by social rank. The emperor, called the Sapa Inca, ruled over everyone and was obeyed without question. He was believed to be a living god, a **descendant** of the sun god, Inti. Next in importance were the nobles. They were the government officials, temple priests, building engineers, and military leaders. The Saba Inca and the nobles had many **privileges**. They lived in stone palaces, had more than one wife, wore beautiful jewelry, and dressed in brightly colored clothes woven for them from the silkiest wool yarns. Most of the common people were farmers. In the highlands of the Andes, they **cultivated** potatoes and maize and looked after herds of llamas and alpacas. The government saw to it that the commoners were given the **necessities** for a simple life. They, in return, were **obliged** to give goods and some form of service to the empire.

    There were many gods and goddesses in the Inca religion. Two of the most important of these were Viracocha, the god of creation, and Inti, the sun god, whose warmth helped crops to ripen. **Sacrifices** of llamas, guinea pigs, and food were regularly made to the gods and goddesses. These offerings, the Incas believed, helped to **avert** troubles, natural disasters, and sickness. Religious festivals were held throughout the year. These took place outdoors, often on large **plazas**. They included singing and dancing to the music of flutes and drums.

    The Incas were skilled in constructing roads and making rope bridges that crossed over rivers and **gorges**. Although travel was by foot, they built thousands of miles of roads that linked together the empire. Relays of runners carried memorized messages along these roads. The Incas also **excelled** in the crafts of weaving, pottery, and metalworking. Many prized objects and ornaments were made from gold, which they called "sweat of the sun."

    In the 1530s, the Spanish came to the empire in search of this gold. They conquered the Incas, destroyed their temples, and took their gold and silver wealth. The great Inca empire was gone forever.

Name: _____   Date: _____

Crossword Puzzle

Complete the puzzle by filling in the vocabulary words that fit the definitions.

Across

5. stretched or continued in a direction
7. offerings to a god
8. special advantages, rights, or favors given to others
9. things that can't be done without
10. public squares in a city or town
11. to keep from happening, prevent

Down

1. helped grow by work and care
2. offspring, person who comes from a certain person or family
3. required to do something for social or legal reasons
4. grew or developed strongly and well
5. was or did better than others
6. narrow valleys between high cliffs

Word Whiz

The word **plaza** came into our language from the Spanish language. Some other words that entered English from Spanish are

rodeo: a contest or show of skills in such things as roping cattle and riding horses
hammock: a swinging bed usually made of canvas or rope and hung by cords at each end
stampede: a sudden scattering and flight of a frightened herd of cattle or horses
bonanza: a source of great profit or wealth
cargo: a load of goods carried on such things as a ship or airplane
patio: a paved area at the back of a house, used for outdoor eating and relaxing
corral: a fenced in place for keeping such animals as horses or cattle

Name: _____   Date: _____

Snakes: Hunters and Hunted

There are over 2,600 different kinds of snakes in the world today. They range in size from small, wormlike creatures to giants that can be more than 20 feet long. Snakes use their strong muscles to **propel** their bodies over the ground, up tree trunks, or through the water. Their long, **flexible** backbones allow them to bend and coil in any direction.

All snakes eat animals. They feed on such prey as lizards, birds, frogs, toads, fish, mice, rabbits, and even other snakes. A snake's sharp sense of smell helps it find food. To explore the area around it, the snake flicks out its tongue and collects odor **particles**. When the tongue returns to its mouth, sensory cells help it identify the odors. Rattlesnakes and some other snakes have pit organs on their heads that can **detect** heat from nearby warm-blooded animals. With this special sense, they can track mammals and birds either day or night.

Poisonous or not, snakes are **formidable** hunters. Some search for prey. Others lie quietly in **ambush** waiting for a meal to come by. Snakes use their sharp teeth to catch and grip animals. They don't chew their prey. Instead, they swallow them whole. Because their upper and lower jaws are loosely connected, they can even swallow meals that are larger than their own heads. Many snakes kill their victims before eating them. Boas and pythons wrap their coils around the body of their prey and then tighten the coils until the animal **suffocates**. Poisonous snakes kill their prey with a poison called venom. Fangs in the snake's upper jaw **inject** this deadly poison into the animal's body.

Snakes are hunted and eaten by a number of animals. To protect themselves, snakes have developed a variety of defenses. Many have colors and patterns that blend in with their surroundings and help them hide. Some poisonous snakes have bright, **conspicuous** colors that warn enemies that they are dangerous and should be left alone. There are harmless snakes that **mimic** the colors and markings of these poisonous snakes so that they, too, will be avoided. Spitting cobras **deter** attacks by spraying venom into the eyes of their attackers. They can shoot this venom out of their fangs for a distance of over six feet. The hognose snake has one of the most unusual ways of defending itself. When an enemy **confronts** it, this nonpoisonous snake puffs itself up, hisses, and strikes with its mouth closed. If this display fails to scare the animal away, it rolls over on its back, opens its mouth, sticks out its tongue, and plays dead.

Name: _____ Date: _____

Crossword Puzzle

Complete the puzzle by filling in the vocabulary words that fit the definitions.

Across

4. easily seen, noticeable
6. place for hiding away while waiting to make a surprise attack
7. dies from lack of oxygen
9. to prevent or discourage from happening
11. easily bent
12. to force a fluid into

Down

1. hard to overcome, causing fear or dread
2. meets face to face in a bold way
3. tiny bits, specks
5. to push or drive forward
8. to discover the presence of something hidden or not easily noticed
10. to imitate or copy closely

Word Whiz

The word **propel** comes from the Latin word *pellere*, which means "to push," or "to drive." Some other words with the word root **-pel** are

expel: to throw or drive out with force, to force to leave
repel: to force or drive back
dispel: to drive away or scatter, make disappear

The word **inject** comes from the Latin word *jacere*, which means "to throw." Some other words with the word root **-ject-** are

projectile: an object made to be shot or thrown with force through the air
trajectory: the curved path followed by such things as a projectile, rocket, or comet

Name: _____   Date: _____

The California Gold Rush

Gold fever! It started on a day in January 1848 when a few nuggets of gold were found in a stream near John Sutter's sawmill. As word of this discovery spread through California, hundreds of men rushed to the area. More and more gold was found in riverbeds, on hills, and in the mountains. News of California's gold traveled east. At first, most people were **skeptical**. More tall tales from the West, they thought. But in December, U.S. President James Polk announced that the reports of gold discoveries had been **verified**. Soon, thousands were headed for California, **lured** by dreams of instant wealth.

For most of these fortune-seekers, traveling to California proved to be an **ordeal**. Those who **trekked** overland by wagon had to cross fast-flowing rivers, brave violent storms, and survive the heat of the desert. Many who lived on the East Coast went to California by ship. Some sailed around South America's Cape Horn. Others took a difficult shortcut across land in Mexico or Panama. Overcrowded sleeping spaces, spoiled food, sickness, and rough seas were just some of the hardships these travelers faced.

Mining camps, with names like You Bet and Last Chance, popped up wherever large quantities of gold were found. These camps were rough and **unruly** places. There were no laws and not many rules. **Disputes** over digging rights often ended in fights. The miners slept in tents or shacks, bathed in streams, and cooked their meals over open fires. In the larger camps, some people **prospered** without digging for gold. Merchants set up stores where they charged **exorbitant** prices for supplies and food. One egg could cost as much as $3. Others opened saloons and hired musicians and entertainers. They charged a pinch of gold for just one swallow of whiskey. In these saloons, some miners **squandered** their gold on liquor and unlucky bets in card games.

By the early 1850s, the miners' backbreaking work was **yielding** less and less gold. Most of the gold that remained was deep in the ground and required heavy equipment to mine it. Many men became **disheartened**. They headed home to their families or looked for jobs in the fast-growing California towns. By the end of the Gold Rush, only a small number of the miners had made quick fortunes. But all of them had taken part in a great adventure that helped shape the growth and development of our country.

Name: _____ Date: _____

Crossword Puzzle

Complete the puzzle by filling in the vocabulary words that fit the definitions.

Across
2. in doubt about the truth of something
5. arguments
8. hard to control or manage
10. traveled slowly and with difficulty
11. producing
12. discouraged

Down
1. difficult or painful experience
3. well above what is usual or reasonable
4. attracted or tempted
6. had success or good fortune, particularly in making or getting money
7. wasted or foolishly spent
9. proved to be true

Word Whiz

The word **disheartened** begins with the prefix **dis-**. This prefix means "not" or "the opposite of." Some other words that start with this prefix are

disobedient: refusing to obey (not obedient)
disloyal: unfaithful (not loyal)
dissimilar: not alike, different (not similar)
disprove: prove false or incorrect (the opposite of prove)
disrespectful: showing no respect or regard for (not respectful)
disconnect: undo or break the connection of (the opposite of connect)

Name: _____   Date: _____

Mammoth Search

Woolly mammoths were hairy, elephantlike animals that roamed the **tundra** between 400,000 and 10,000 years ago. During this time, mammoths sometimes fell through ice or into mud pits and couldn't escape. Their bodies were then sealed in frozen ground called **permafrost**. Permafrost can keep a mammoth's body intact for thousands of years. This frozen ground keeps **bacteria** inactive so they won't rot the body. As a result, scientists have been able to find mammoth fossils that are in excellent condition.

In 2003, scientists in the Yukagir region of Siberia found such a mammoth **fossil**. Not only were much of the animal's hair and bones still present, but it also had a complete head. Even some of the brain **tissue**, an eye, and the ears were intact. Sometimes, scientists have discovered food from a mammoth's last meal still inside the animal. The remains of leaves, grasses, and twigs were found inside the stomach of the Yukagir mammoth. Scientists estimate that these **massive** herbivores ate about 600 pounds of plants a day. Because plants usually prefer **milder** climates and softer soil, it's natural to wonder how the mammoths were able to find so much food in such a cold region. Some scientists think that the tundra looked much different thousands of years ago. When the mammoths lived, the tundra received little rain or snow. During the summer, the upper layer of permafrost melted, allowing many species of plants to grow. This provided lots of green goodies for the mammoths. Another belief is that mammoths **migrated** south during the cold, dark winter months, to a slightly warmer **climate** where plants grew year-round.

Scientists aren't sure which explanation is correct. But new technology is being developed that will help mammoth hunters unlock these and other mammoth mysteries. To study frozen mammoths, scientists once **thawed** fossils and cut them open. But there were many problems with this method. For example, **defrosting** mammoths often dried them out. As a result, muscle, skin, and organs were destroyed. Valuable material that could have provided clues about the mammoths was lost. But today, scientists in Japan use a special computer to see what's inside the Yukagir mammoth. This way they can study the animal without destroying it.

Hopefully, this new technology will also allow scientists to uncover the greatest mammoth mystery of all: why these animals died out. Some scientists believe that rising temperatures made it too warm for the mammoths to survive. Others believe that overhunting by early humans is to blame. Though many **theories** exist, there is one thing that is certain: Today's mammoth hunters won't rest until they have the answers.

Crossword Puzzle

Complete the puzzle by filling in the vocabulary words that fit the definitions.

Across

2. a cold, treeless, usually flat area in the far North
4. a layer of permanently frozen soil
8. a mass of cells that form a particular animal part
9. melted
10. extremely large
11. the hardened remains of a plant or animal that lived long ago
12. traveled from one place to another and back again, at regular times each year

Down

1. ideas that explain how or why something happens
3. thawing out an item that is frozen
5. not too harsh
6. organisms too small to be seen by the naked eye
7. the average temperature and rainfall of an area over many years

Word Whiz

Mammoth is another word for "huge." Some other adjectives that describe something huge are

enormous, gigantic, giant, colossal, gargantuan, and **massive.**

An antonym for "mammoth" is **minute.** Some synonyms for something minute are

miniature, microscopic, diminutive, infinitesimal, and **wee.**

An American Hero

In 1919, Richard Orteig offered a $25,000 prize to the first pilot to fly nonstop between New York and Paris. Seven years later, this money had not yet been won. But airplane engines were becoming more powerful and interest in the contest was heating up. In early 1927, several serious **contenders** for the prize were making plans to try to fly across the Atlantic. One of these was a 25 year old named Charles Lindbergh.

Lindbergh had gained a **reputation** as a fearless and skilled pilot. He had earned money doing daredevil stunts in his own small plane, graduated first in his class from a U.S. Army flight-training school, and flown mail in all kinds of weather between St. Louis and Chicago. Now, he had **resolved** to win the Orteig prize.

In April, an aircraft manufacturer in San Diego, California, was finishing the construction of the single-engine plane that Lindbergh had helped to design. This was the airplane in which he would try to reach Paris. Lindbergh believed that it was **essential** to keep the plane as light as possible so that he could carry more than 400 gallons of fuel. To keep all other weight to a **minimum**, he would not take a radio or a parachute. He would even sit in a lightweight wicker chair instead of the usual leather pilot's seat. Lindbergh named his plane Spirit of St. Louis to honor his **sponsors** in St. Louis, Missouri, who had paid for the plane.

At 7:52 A.M. on May 22, 1927, Lindbergh took off from Roosevelt Field in New York, carrying a rubber raft, charts, maps, a bag of sandwiches, and water. As the plane began its **ascent** into the sky, it barely cleared the telephone wires at the edge of the field. He kept to his course, flying through thick fogs, winds, and an ice storm. He stretched his arms and legs to **alleviate** the aches in his cramped muscles. But Lindbergh's worst enemy was **fatigue**. Hour after hour, he struggled to keep his eyes open. Finally, he sighted the lights of Paris and, with great relief, landed his plane at Le Bourget Field. He had flown more than 3,600 miles in 33.5 hours.

An **exuberant** crowd greeted Lindbergh at the airport with loud cheers and shouts. He had won the Orteig prize and made the world's first **solo**, nonstop flight across the Atlantic. When he returned to the United States, he was honored with celebrations, awards, and a huge parade in New York City. Lindbergh had become a **celebrity** whose heroic flight and amazing courage excited people all over the world.

Name: _____ Date: _____

Crossword Puzzle

Complete the puzzle by filling in the vocabulary words that fit the definitions.

Across

4. people or a group who supports someone
6. lively, full of spirit
8. those who compete in a contest
9. to relieve, ease, make more bearable
10. weariness, tiredness
11. the act of going up, climbing, rising

Down

1. least possible amount
2. very important, necessary
3. what people generally think about a person
4. done by one person
5. famous or well-known person
7. made up one's mind, decided

Word Whiz

Homophones are words that sound alike but have different spellings and meanings.
Ascent and **assent** are homophones.
Assent means "to agree, to give consent."
Some other homophones are

compliment: something good said about someone
complement: something that completes something or makes it perfect
stationery: paper and envelopes used for writing letters
stationary: having a fixed place, not moving
alter: to change the appearance of, make different
altar: a stand or table or raised area used for religious worship

Narratives Word List

abolished (40)
absorb (16)
abundant (30)
accentuate (30)
acclaim (24)
accommodate (6)
accompanied (24)
accomplishments (24)
acknowledging (18)
acquired (42)
adjacent (26)
affectionately (28)
affluent (40)
affordable (28)
agile (8)
alleviate (54)
ambush (48)
ancestors (30)
appalled (44)
aptitude (44)
archaeologist (26)
artifacts (42)
ascent (54)
aspired (42)
assets (8)
astonished (26)
astound (8)
atmosphere (16)
attained (32)
attired (38)
audible (14)
avert (46)
awed (44)
bacteria (52)

benefits (34)
blanketed (16)
boisterous (6)
bustling (38)
camouflage (20)
carcass (38)
cauldrons (38)
celebrity (54)
century (38)
climate (52)
clumped (16)
collaborate (18)
colonies (20)
commemorate (30)
commenced (6)
commend (40)
components (28)
concealed (40)
conclude (6)
condense (16)
confronts (48)
congested (28)
congregate (42)
conscientious (10)
consecutive (32)
conserve (44)
conspicuous (48)
consumed (38)
contaminate (20)
contemporary (28)
contenders (54)
cope (16)
correspondent (18)
crevices (20)

cultivated (46)
dangerous (16)
debris (12)
deceased (30)
deceit (20)
defrosting (52)
dense (10)
depicts (24)
descendant (46)
designated (44)
destination (42)
detect (48)
deter (48)
deteriorated (30)
devours (10)
diligently (36)
disguised (40)
disheartened (50)
dismantled (12)
disputes (50)
dissolves (34)
dissuaded (18)
distinction (32)
distressed (40)
diverse (12)
doze (10)
dramatize (8)
drought (18)
duration (42)
dwell (20)
dynamic (32)
edible (36)
efficiently (28)
elaborate (36)

Narratives Word List (Continued)

elated (18)	formidable (48)	jostled (14)
elevated (38)	fossil (52)	jut (34)
emerged (8)	fulfilled (18)	legends (22)
employer (32)	garments (6)	limestone (34)
encounter (6)	gestures (10)	linger (22)
endeavored (32)	gorges (46)	looted (26)
endured (42)	gradually (34)	lured (50)
engaged (32)	grime (6)	lurk (20)
enrolled (44)	grove (44)	manipulate (42)
ensure (36)	habitat (10)	marveled (28)
erected (30)	hazardous (22)	massive (52)
essential (54)	host (30)	matinees (14)
evading (20)	hostile (22)	microbes (34)
evaporates (16)	humiliate (30)	migrated (52)
exaggerate (40)	ignited (28)	migration (24)
excavating (26)	illuminate (14)	milder (52)
excelled (46)	immense (36)	mimic (48)
excursions (28)	immigrated (42)	mineral (34)
exhausted (22)	impression (26)	minimum (54)
exhibitions (24)	incredible (32)	moist (16)
exorbitant (50)	infection (34)	molten (18)
expenditure (12)	inflate (20)	morsels (38)
extended (46)	ingenious (44)	necessities (46)
extinction (16)	inhabit (12)	novices (42)
extinguished (12)	initial (14)	numerous (24)
extricated (8)	inject (48)	obliged (46)
exuberant (54)	injustice (24)	obtained (40)
fashion (36)	installed (12)	opponents (32)
fatigue (54)	intact (8)	opulent (26)
flexible (48)	intended (26)	ordeal (50)
flourished (46)	intense (18)	originated (42)
foliage (36)	interior (12)	ornate (6)
forage (10)	intimidating (10)	particles (48)
formations (34)	jeered (14)	perilous (24)

Narratives Word List (Continued)

permafrost (52)
persevering (28)
persisted (26)
pierces (36)
placid (10)
plazas (46)
plight (10)
portrait (42)
precaution (22)
predators (36)
premiere (18)
preserve (20)
previous (28)
privileges (46)
proficient (30)
profusion (26)
prohibited (14)
propel (48)
prospered (50)
pungent (38)
pursue (8)
quest (24)
rambunctious (12)
ravenous (38)
recipient (40)
recline (6)
recounted (30)
recuperating (44)
reigned (26)
renovation (12)
renowned (8)
replenished (38)
reputation (54)
resemble (36)

reserve (16)
resolved (54)
resounded (8)
resume (22)
retained (12)
revered (32)
route (22)
sacrifices (46)
schemes (40)
seeped (34)
shrewdly (40)
siblings (24)
simulate (14)
situated (14)
skeptical (50)
slaughtered (18)
solo (54)
spectators (32)
sponsors (54)
squandered (50)
stalactites (34)
stalagmites (34)
stamina (22)
strenuous (6)
stroll (6)
submerged (8)
suffocates (48)
summits (44)
sumptuous (38)
supremacy (10)
survivors (32)
suspending (36)
symbols (12)
tedious (26)

teem (20)
thawed (52)
theories (52)
tiers (14)
tissue (52)
tranquil (20)
transmits (28)
transported (22)
trekked (50)
tribute (44)
tundra (52)
undaunted (22)
unruly (50)
unwary (14)
unwieldy (30)
utilize (36)
vanished (8)
vapor (16)
vegetation (10)
vendors (6)
venture (22)
verified (50)
versatile (14)
vivid (24)
vowed (40)
withering (18)
yearning (44)
yielding (50)

Word Whiz Word List

- acrobat (15)
- allocated (45)
- allocation (45)
- altar (55)
- alter (55)
- amateur (15)
- aquanaut (21)
- aquarium (21)
- aquatic (21)
- aqueduct (21)
- archaeology (27)
- assent (55)
- aviary (37)
- aviation (37)
- aviator (37)
- benefactor (35)
- beneficial (35)
- bonanza (47)
- brutalize (9)
- careful (17)
- cargo (47)
- carnivore (11)
- centennial (39)
- colossal (53)
- collide (19)
- compatible (19)
- compile (19)
- complement (55)
- compliment (55)
- confer (19)
- conservation (45)
- consolidate (19)
- convene (19)
- corral (47)
- covert (41)
- cryptographer (41)
- debut (15)
- decade (39)
- decapod (39)
- decathlon (39)
- defines (45)
- definition (45)
- detour (15)
- diminutive (53)
- disconnect (51)
- disloyal (51)
- dismiss (29)
- disobedient (51)
- dispel (49)
- disprove (51)
- disrespectful (51)
- dissimilar (51)
- diurnal (11)
- donated (45)
- donation (45)
- eavesdrop (41)
- emigrated (43)
- emissary (29)
- emit (29)
- enormous (53)
- equalize (9)
- espionage (41)
- excluded (43)
- expel (49)
- exports (43)
- fantasize (9)
- fearful (17)
- fledgling (37)
- frigid (7)
- furious (17)
- gargantuan (53)
- geology (27)
- giant (53)
- gigantic (53)
- hammock (47)
- herbivore (11)
- hopeful (17)
- humorous (17)
- illegible (31)
- illiterate (31)
- immobile (31)
- imports (43)
- imprecise (31)
- inaccurate (25)
- included (43)
- incompetent (25)
- ineligible (25)
- infinitesimal (53)
- insectivore (11)
- insignificant (25)
- inspect (33)
- insufficient (25)
- intrigue (15)
- involuntary (25)
- irrelevant (31)
- irretrievable (31)
- kaleidoscope (33)
- malady (35)
- malevolent (35)
- malfunction (35)
- malign (35)
- mammoth (53)

Word Whiz Word List (Continued)

marine (21)
mariner (21)
massive (53)
meteorology (27)
microscope (33)
microscopic (53)
millennium (39)
miniature (53)
minute (53)
missile (29)
nestling (37)
nocturnal (11)
omit (29)
omnivorous (11)
painful (17)
paleontology (27)
patio (47)
periscope (33)
plumage (37)
postwar (23)
powerful (17)
predate (23)
predetermine (23)
preen (37)
prehistoric (23)
premature (23)
preview (23)
projectile (49)
psychology (27)
purify (9)
quotation (45)
quoted (45)
readmit (13)
redistribute (13)

reevaluate (13)
reinsert (13)
remit (29)
reoccur (13)
repel (49)
reunite (13)
rodeo (47)
scald (7)
scavenger (11)
simplify (9)
souvenir (15)
spacious (17)
spectacle (33)
spectacles (33)
stampede (47)
stationary (55)
stationery (55)
submit (29)
successful (17)
surveillance (41)
talons (37)
telescope (33)
tepid (7)
thermal (7)
thermometer (7)
thermostat (7)
trajectory (49)
verbalize (9)
vibrates (45)
vibration (45)
vigorous (17)
voluminous (17)
wee (53)
zoology (27)

Answers

Ancient Roman Baths (Page 7)

Harry Houdini: Master of Escape (Page 9)

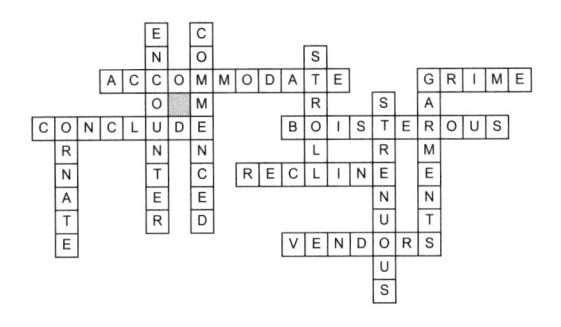

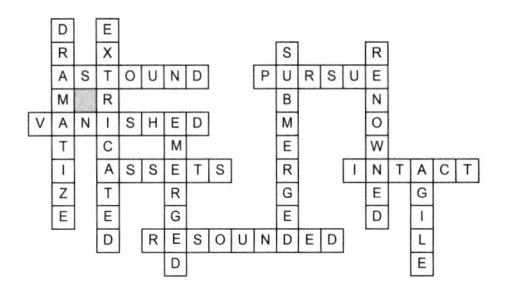

Mountain Gorillas (Page 11)

The White House (Page 13)

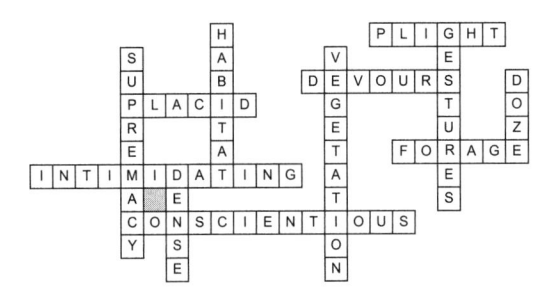

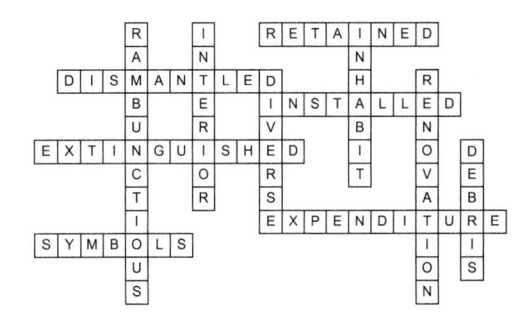

The Globe Theater (Page 15)

Disappearing Frogs (Page 17)

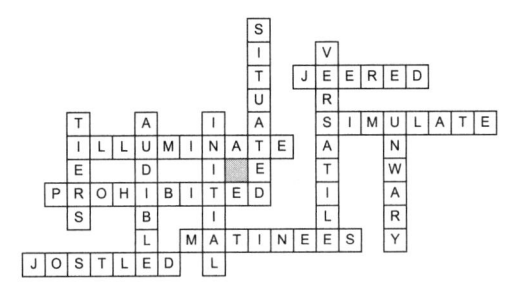

Margaret Bourke-White (Page 19)

Life on Coral Reefs (Page 21)

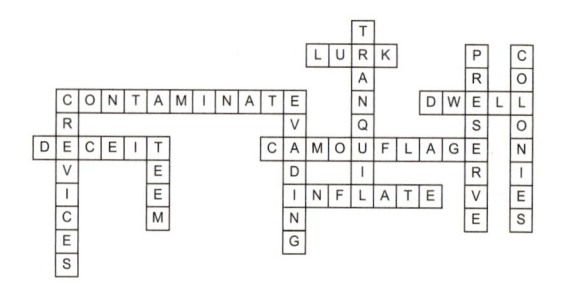

The Pony Express (Page 23)

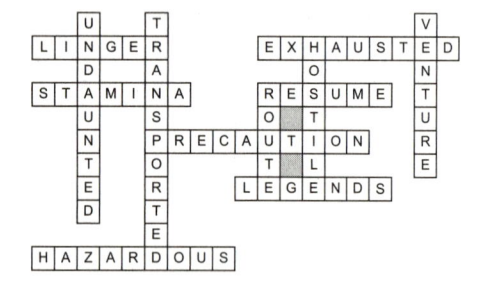

The Story Painter (Page 25)

Treasures of Tutankhamun (Page 27)

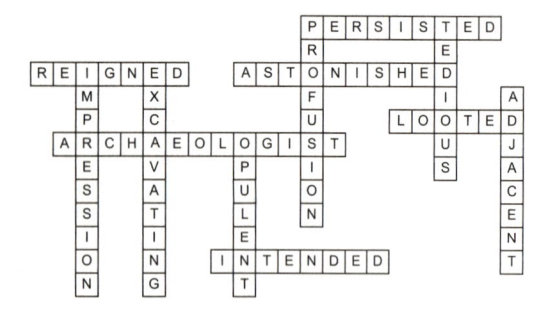

The Tin Lizzie (Page 29)

Totem Poles (Page 31)

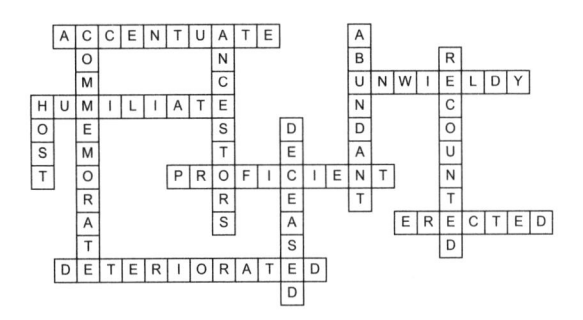

Across: ACCENTUATE, HUMILIATE, UNWIELDY, PROFICIENT, ERECTED, DETERIORATED
Down: COMMEMORATE, HOST, ANCESTORS, ABUNDANT, ACCOUNT, DEFEATED, REVERED

Roberto Clemente (Page 33)

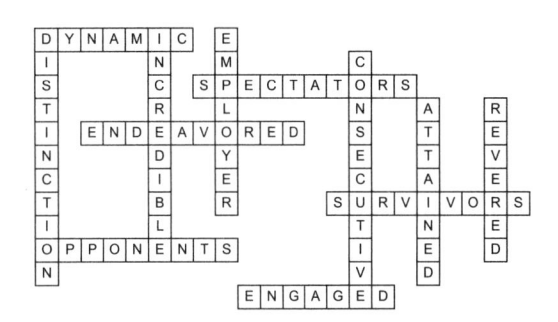

Across: DYNAMIC, SPECTATORS, ENDEAVORED, SURVIVORS, OPPONENTS, ENGAGED
Down: DISTINCTION, EMERGENCY, INCREDIBLY, CONSECUTIVE, ATTAINED, REVERED

Journey Into the Earth (Page 35)

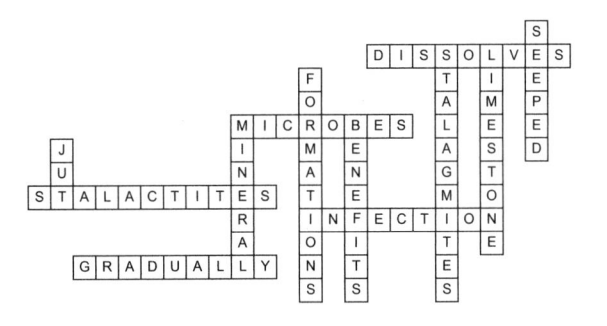

Across: DISSOLVES, MICROBES, STALACTITES, INFECTION, GRADUALLY
Down: SUSPENDED, FORMATIONS, INANIMATE, JUT, STALAGMITES, DEPOSITS

Bird Nests (Page 37)

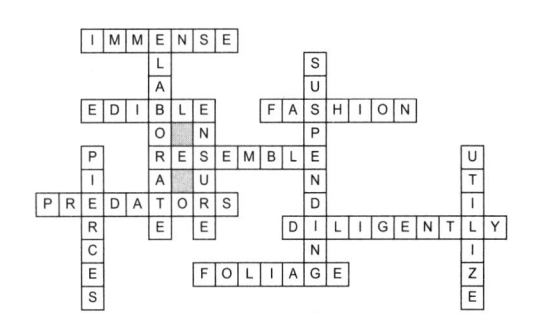

Across: IMMENSE, EDIBLE, FASHION, RESEMBLE, PREDATORS, DILIGENTLY, FOLIAGE
Down: LAYLON, SUSPENDED, PIECES, UTILIZE

A Medieval Feast (Page 39)

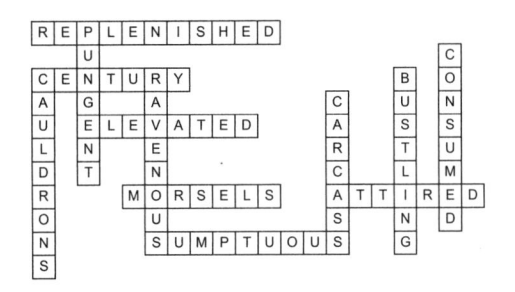

Across: REPLENISHED, CENTURY, ELEVATED, MORSELS, ATTIRED, SUMPTUOUS
Down: AUGMENT, PAGEANT, BUSTLING, CARCASS, CONSUMS, BOULDRONS

"Crazy Bet": A Civil War Spy (Page 41)

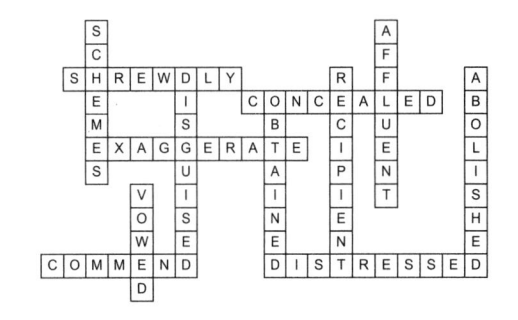

Across: SHREWDLY, CONCEALED, EXAGGERATE, COMMEND, DISTRESSED
Down: SCHEME, AFFLUENT, RECIPIENT, ABOLISHED, VOWS, ISSUE, CABINET

History of the Yo-Yo (Page 43)

A Man of the Wilderness (Page 45)

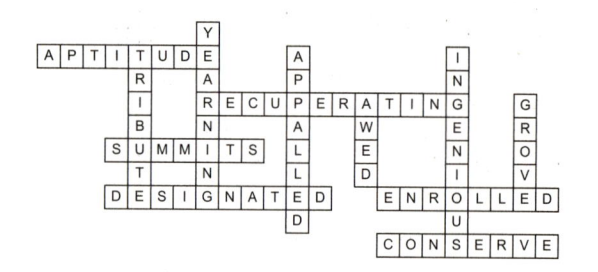

The Incas (Page 47)

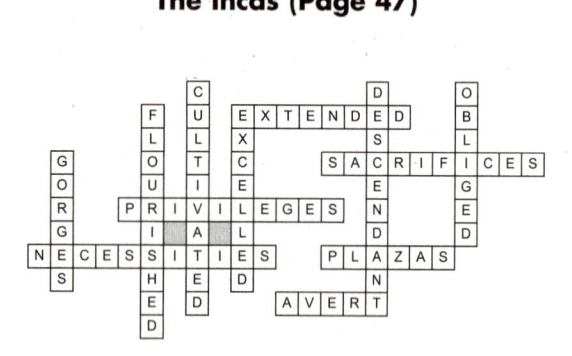

Snakes: Hunters and Hunted (Page 49)

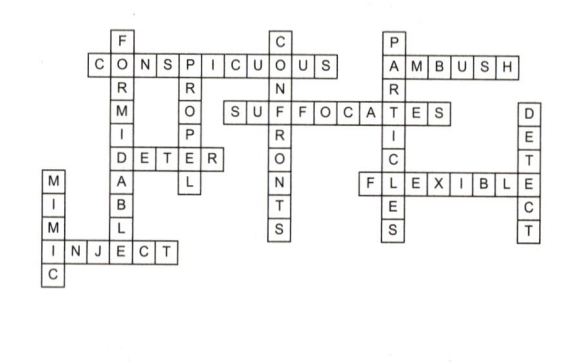

The California Gold Rush (Page 51)

Mammoth Search (Page 53)